NOT
EVERY
WOMAN

NOT EVERY WOMAN

*Questions Answered
By Women 40 Plus Years Old,
Never Married, And Childless*

Lauretta E. Joyner

ReadersMagnet, LLC

Not Every Woman
Copyright © 2022 by Lauretta E Joyner

Published in the United States of America
ISBN   Paperback: 978-1-959761-28-0
ISBN   eBook: 978-1-959761-29-7

All rights reserved. No part of this publication may be reproduced, stored in a retrieval system or transmitted in any way by any means, electronic, mechanical, photocopy, recording or otherwise without the prior permission of the author except as provided by USA copyright law.

The opinions expressed by the author are not necessarily those of ReadersMagnet, LLC.

ReadersMagnet, LLC
10620 Treena Street, Suite 230 | San Diego, California, 92131 USA
1.619. 354. 2643 | www.readersmagnet.com

Book design copyright © 2022 by ReadersMagnet, LLC. All rights reserved.

Cover design by Ericka Obando
Interior design by Dorothy Lee

Table of Contents

Dedication 7
Introduction 9
Stats 11
Stereotypes 13
Outside The Box—We Are Different! Embrace It! 15
What If? 16
Why Me? 17
It Is What It Is! You Better Be Happy Girl! 19
Talk About Old Maids! 21
Real Women, Real Talk From The Ladies! 22
Afterthought 254
Bibliography 256

DEDICATION

I dedicate this book first to Jesus Christ, who placed in me this awesome idea to write on this topic. Secondly, to all women everywhere who are a part of this glorious group, particularly those who have contributed to this book. Thirdly, thank you to everyone who helped to make this book a reality. Also, to anyone who is open-minded and willing to look at a different perspective- even if you may not fully understand or agree with it.

INTRODUCTION

I am writing this book to provide a new or different perspective on a group of women that is seldom heard from, if not even fully known about. I must admit even researching statistical information on this group was indeed challenging. Particularly, if you are looking for information on not only single women over 40, but also who have never been married, and have no children- research is few and far between. This goes to show that this is truly a taboo subject. However, God has led me to write this book to let the world know that we in this category are everywhere, and we are beautiful, successful, strong, loving, and courageous women. Yes, we are unique in our current situations in life. I say that because the status of being unmarried and child-free, does not mean that it's always going to be that way. Whenever the time is right, (meaning the right man for them comes along), a woman may marry. If God allows her to physically have a child or children, she will, if she cannot physically have a child, but wants to embark on a journey of motherhood, there are other options like adoption and foster care. Other women don't want to get married or have children at all. Some women are very content in being single with no children and there is absolutely nothing wrong with that. Many times, due to societal pressures and expectations ingrained in us from childhood, we naturally assume that women are all programmed with a desire to be a wife and a mother. We may particularly assume that unmarried women over 40 years old are desperate to get married and have children. There may be some women who feel that way, who are worried about their biological clocks, yet they want to be married first. Thereby, having the right man may not be the easiest thing to achieve to get the process started. But many other women are at peace with waiting on their time to marry and if not, they are not going to lose their minds. Many are leading successful and full lives and are content, while others are not. In the coming chapters, you will see what some women have to say on the topic of wanting to get married or not. It was very important for me to give a voice and an outlet to these women who we rarely get to hear from firsthand.

STATS

Let's talk stats! According to the U.S. Census:
- Women who were never married went from 20% to about 30% from 1950-2020.[1]
- In 2014: One in seven women aged 40-44, have not had any children nor marries (Rybinska and Morgan, 2019).[2]
- Percent of women in their late 40's (45-49), who had never been married 2010[3]

Worldwide	4.3%
Australia and New Zealand	14.1%
Latin American and Caribbean	13.4%
Europe and North America	10.8%
Sub-Saharan Africa	6.1%
Northern Africa and Western Asia	4.8%
Oceania (excluding Australia and New Zealand)	3.7%
Eastern and South-Eastern Asia	2.5%
Central and Southern Asia	1.1%

- Marital Status of the U.S. Population (Female) in 2020 by sex (in millions)[4]

---

1. United States Census Bureau, Decennial Census, 1950 to 1990, and Current Population Survey, Annual Social and Economic Supplements, 1993 to 2021.
2. Rybinska, A., and Morgan, S.P. (2019) Childless expectations and childlessness over the life course. Social Force. 97(4), 1571-1602.
3. *https://www.psychologytoday.com/us/blog/living-single/201908/around-the-world-marriage-is-declining-singles-are rising.*
4. https://www.statistica.com/statistics/242030/marital-status-of-the-US-population-by-sex.

NEVER MARRIED 40.87

- In the U.S., 1 in 5 women reach the end of their childbearing years without having given birth compared to one-in-ten in the 1970's.[5]

---

[5] Cohn, D., and Livingstone, G. (2020, July 31). Childlessness up among all women; Down among women with advanced degrees. Pew Research Center's Social and Demographic Trends Project. *https://www.pewresearch.org/social-trends/2010/06/25* childlessness-up-among-all-women-down-among-all-women-down-among-women-with-advanced-degrees/.

STEREOTYPES

Many of the women in this group have likely had someone say something to them in bad taste even though their intentions were not to be insulting. Of course, there are stereotypes for women in this group. I know you've heard the story of the single, old woman with 50 cats, portraying that the woman is lonely, and the only family she has are an absurd number of cats. Now, I am not trying to offend someone who loves cats. There is certainly nothing wrong with having pets.

I have had people react with shock and surprise when I told them I have never been married, and I have no children. I remember telling someone I have never been married, and they exclaimed, "You have NEVER been married?", as if that was too unbelievable to comprehend. Some people just can't fathom that you can get to this age and have never been married and have no children. You can almost see the wheels turning in their heads and their thought processes. It's like their thinking, there's got to be something wrong with her. Once a gentleman said to me, "Why are you not married, there's nothing wrong with you is there?" Well, after hearing that I was stunned for a few seconds, then snapped out of it to reply simply, "No, there is nothing wrong with me.", and let it go at that. The root of the problem is that many people don't understand what they don't know or haven't experienced themselves.

That is why I am writing this book to give people an insight into this demographic of women. I want to give a perspective on a subject that most people may not understand or have previously thought about. This book is not meant to be the be all end all book on this subject—it's just my take on it. I specifically wanted to write about women who are at least 40 because 40 is a major turning point in a woman's life. For women, it can be the countdown time for having children. It's a turning point because you are no longer considered a young adult—your middle-aged. For the most part, this is usually (by societal terms), an age where a woman would have either been married or had a child.

OUTSIDE THE BOX—WE ARE DIFFERENT! EMBRACE IT!

Does society generally favor married women with children in general? Yes! (In my opinion). That's because of our societal history (particularly in the United States where the nuclear family is prevalent in all advertising, entertainment, and more. Marriage and children can of course be beautiful things, but there is also no obligation for every woman to subscribe to the norm.

Now I won't paint a picture of women who are at least 40 years old unmarried, childless women as sad, or pathetic. Quite the contrary! Women in this group are courageous, happy, and in many cases, content. They are career-focused, goal oriented, and mentors, whose footprint on this planet is needed.

This book is not a pity party, woe is me book so that people can say "Oh poor thing—that is so sad." I want this book to uplift and highlight this group of women, just as much as looking at some of the negative that may come along with this demographic.

WHAT IF?

What would my life be like if I were married and had children much earlier in my life? I am sure many women in this group have asked this question in reflection many times over their lives. Much of this introspection comes from watching their peers and comparing themselves to other women who have their own families. As much as some would not want to admit it, we do sometimes look at women who are married with children as the grass being greener on the other side, particularly, for women who desire to be married and have children. So, with pretty much anything in life if we desire something and we give thought to what we want, the question of What if? may come up.

WHY ME?

Why am I 40+ years old and still not married and childless? Is there something wrong with me? Am I ever going to be married with kids? Or am I going to be single and childless for the rest of my life? What did I do to deserve this? When we start comparing ourselves to other women, we say things like, "I am a good person, I have a great job/career that I love, I have a degree, etc. Why me?" or "I see other women who treat their marriage like a game or a joke and mishandle/mistreat their child(ren), and yet and still they go on with what appears as no problems." Reasonable women in this group have questioned themselves and questioned God. I have spoken with women who had their plans dead set on being married and having children way before reaching the age of 40.

Even though the question Why me? is asked, there may be many answers to that question. An answer maybe because that it's not in God's plan (at least not yet for some). There may be some things that the woman must fulfill first. This may be purpose or a career goal, or it may be that a person needs to grow in a particular area of character or overcome past trauma. We may be so used to being on our own and doing things our way, that we may not be willing to change that. Let's face it: Being married and on top of that, having children, does require sacrifice and being selfless. However, it could also mean that a woman has made a decision that took them on a different path than marrying and having kids.

In the vein of this common saying, "Delay does not mean denial." Every woman sets her timeline on when she wants something to happen. You may have things planned and mapped out to a T, but life may not follow that road map. Even if it never happens, we must live with it.

Being a woman who has reached 40 and has never been married or had kids is not a death sentence. You can be a mentor to other children out there that need love and guidance, or find purpose through career advancement, starting a business, and following lifelong dreams. This world has so many problems and as a single woman with no children, you are blessed to have the time and the will to change this world to make it a better place in your way. Your contribution does not have to be large to make a big difference. Realistically for some, it may mean you may never get married and have children. And that's okay. We can't live the rest of our lives in regret, but we must live our lives in purpose and making positive changes.

IT IS WHAT IT IS!
YOU BETTER BE HAPPY GIRL!

In life, we must walk the path that God has given us. The question is what will we do with what God has given us, and how will we walk our path? I am sure among women of this group; some have come to realize that they may never get married and may never have children. Who says you can't live a fulfilling, happy, joyful, and purposeful life without having a family of your own? There are so many other things in life that are just as important. While some face struggles of infertility or difficulty obtaining "the one," others have simply chosen to be single and child-free. Instead of worrying about other people's opinions, women should feel comfortable with who they are.

I believe that it's never too late to have a family. I've seen and heard of women who didn't get married until they were in their 60's and above. If it's meant to be, it will be. Don't force it. Don't be depressed over it. Don't be jealous of someone who is married and has kids. Most definitely, don't compare yourself to others because you are no less than anyone else because everyone has their own life to live. Everyone is special in God's eyes because God makes each person with a mind, purpose, and will. It's what you do with those things that count. Don't allow people with small and ignorant mindsets to infiltrate your spirit and your mindset. Live life to its fullest utilizing whatever gifts or talents that God has bestowed upon you to help others and make this world a better place to live. So, what if you don't have your own children? If you want to make a positive impact in the lives of children, you can be a mentor or foster mother to children in need. When looking for ways to make your life fulfilling, do it for your own well-being, which in turn will reflect onto others. For some of you, you may be having so much fun and enjoying your life, that you don't even focus on not being married and having a family of your own. Your focus shifts to having internal peace and fulfilling your destiny. To that, I say," You go miss lady!".

TALK ABOUT OLD MAIDS!

Here are some definitions and historical anecdotes that have been used to describe the types of women who are the subject of this book.

The term old maid was 1st used circa 1530. A definition of "Old Maid" by Merriam-Webster (noun)—A woman who has never been married and who is no longer young.[6]

Another similar term related to "Old Maid" is spinster. According to Merriam-Webster it is: An unmarried woman and especially one past the common age for marrying; a woman who seems unlikely to marry.[7]

Many people grew up hearing the phrase "Old Maid"—there's even a children's card game based around trying to avoid ending up with the Old Maid card in hand. There's a picture in our minds of an older woman who has no husband or children and is lonely. She is kind of looked upon as strange, awkward, and an outsider. This stereotype is highly outdated of course, as it is statistically more common for women to remain unmarried and childless in the modern age. But even in the modern day, there still seems to be a stigma that's attached to women of this group.

---

[6] Source: "Old Maid." Merriam-Webster.com Dictionary, Merriam-Webster, *https://www.merriam-webster.com/dictionary/old%20maid*.

[7] *www.Merriam-Webster.com/dictionary/spinster*. From: "spinster definition. Merriam-Webster. Retrieved 5 June 2014.

REAL WOMEN, REAL TALK FROM THE LADIES!

I was curious to know how women of this group felt. These women were asked numerous questions through a 37-question survey. The women are anonymous. The purpose of this survey was to attain the uniqueness of each answer to the questions and to protect the privacy of these women because of the sensitive nature of the questions.

These women are so amazing! Reading the responses impressed me, some saddened me, but many inspired me even more to be thankful of the life that God has given me. I won't take it for granted. This is a blessed life. It was very important that the women who answered these questions be truthful and candid. They did not have to try to impress anyone. If they were happy with this lifestyle, great, and if not, that's okay too. There is no right or wrong answer. It's simply their viewpoint and I highly respect that.

Now it's time to visit the interviews concerning the women who are 40 and over have never been married, and are without children, and their answers to the questionnaire. Not all questions were answered by each woman, however, the questions were answered from each woman's heart and their truth.

1. Name: Leah P.
2. Country: United States.
3. City and/or state: Hawaii.
4. Are you happy/satisfied with being single? Yes.
5. Are you happy/satisfied with not having any children? Yes, I am happy satisfied.
6. Do you or have you ever envied other women who are married and have a child(ren)? Never.
7. When you let others know that you have never been married and have no children, what was their response? What was your response to their response? I don't discuss with strangers or people who are not close to me.
8. What have you learned about being single with no kids? Life is surely fun.
9. What advice do you have for other women 40 and over who have never been married and never had children? It's fine to enjoy being single.
10. For those of you that don't ever want to get married or have children, have you encountered any negativity or criticism about this decision? No.
11. Do you have any regrets? No.
12. Do you choose to be single with no kids or is it circumstantial? Please explain. I choose to be single.
13. Have you ever ruined or sabotaged an opportunity to get married/engaged, because of fear of rejection, commitment, or another reason? No.
14. If your answer is "Yes" above, please explain. N/A
15. Do you feel pressured to get married and have a family from outside sources? (ex., family, church, friends, society, etc.)? No.
16. Have you ever felt embarrassed about being over 40, never been married and without kids? No.

17. Have you had a conversation with God about your situation? No.
18. How do you feel about waiting on God to send you the right husband? Nature will have its way.
19. Do you believe you would have already been married by now? Why? How? No, I don't believe.
20. Are you okay if you never get married and have children? Do you accept this? Are you content? Why? I'm OK.
21. What advice or words of wisdom would you give to other women in general whether single or not, with kids or not? Find a hobby you love.
22. Have you ever been tempted to get married or have a child because you got tired of waiting and you felt time was running out? Give examples. Not yet.
23. Have you ever been engaged or thought you were going to get married and realize it was going to be a big mistake? What happened? Never.
24. Give examples of how you respond to people who question you as to why you're not married. To focus on their marriages.
25. Have you ever thought about what it would be like to be married with children? Never in my mind.
26. Have you ever sabotaged a relationship/dating because you were afraid of getting married/commitment? If so, explain. Never.
27. Are you afraid of getting married? If so, why or for what reason(s)? If not, why or for what reason(s)? Not afraid, but marriage is not my thing.
28. Have you been in a position where you were in a relationship or engaged to please others even though you knew in your heart that was not the right person for you? No.
29. Have you considered adopting child (ren)?, foster care or some other means if you never give birth to any child(ren) of your own? If so, what option did you consider and why? Neither option.
30. Do you need healing or to come to terms of some pains from the past before you can be open to getting married? No.

31. Have you ever tried online dating to find a mate? If so, what was that experience like? I haven't tried online dating. How is it anyway?

32. Looking back, would you do anything differently? If so, please explain. If not, please explain. I am proud of my past and there's nothing I would change about it.

33. For those of you that want to get married, what qualities do you want in a spouse? N/A

34. Should a woman who is at least 40 years old who dates, be dating for the purpose of getting married? No.

35. How are you living your best life? Focusing on my career life for growth.

36. Name some accomplishments, goals, or visions you aspire to complete, have completed, or are working on. I am currently the Director general at a franchise company.

37. Is there anything else you would like to say on the subject (being a woman who is at least 40 years old have never been married before, with no children)? Never judge a book by its cover. You never know their story.

1. Name: Zoe M.
2. Country: USA
3. City and/or State: Hawaii
4. Are you happy/satisfied with being single?
Yes.
5. Are you happy/satisfied with not having any children?
Yes, I am happy/satisfied.
6. Do you or have you ever envied other women who are married and have a child(ren)? No.
7. When you let others know that you have never been married and have no children, what was their response? What was your response to their response? (They) laugh at me, I get angry.

8. What have you learned about being single, with no kids? It is boring.

9. What advice do you have for other women 40 and over, who have never been married and never had children? It is never too late.

10. For those of you that don't ever want to get married or have children, have you encountered any negativity or criticism about this decision? Yes.

11. Do you have any regrets? Yes.

12. Do you choose to be single, with no kids, or is it circumstantial? Please explain. I choose to be single.

13. Have you ever ruined or sabotaged an opportunity to get married/engaged, because of (fear of rejection, commitment, or another reason)? No.

14. If your answer is "Yes" above please explain. N/A

15. Do you feel pressured to get married and have a family from outside sources (ex., family, church, friends, society, etc.)? Maybe.

16. Have you ever felt embarrassed about being over 40 and never been married and no kids? Maybe.

17. Have you had a conversation with God about your situation? Maybe.

18. How do you feel about waiting on God to send you the right husband? God rewards where there is effort.

19. Do you believe you would have already been married by now? Why? How? Yes, if I had my goals focused on getting married.

20. Are you okay if you never get married and have children? Do you accept this? Are you content? Why? Yes, I am content. I am living my best life and achieving my targets.

21. What advice or words of wisdom would you give to other women in general (whether single or not, with kids or not)? If you want a man with a car, you will find him where you have yours parked.

22. Have you ever been tempted to get married or have a child because you got tired of waiting and you felt time was running out? Give examples. No.

23. Have you been engaged or thought you were going to get married and realized it was going to be a big mistake? What happened? I have never been engaged.
24. Give examples of how you respond to people who question you as to why you're not married? I ask the aspects in life they think they are better than me whether financially or well-being.
25. Have you ever thought about what it would be like to be married with children? No.
26. Have you ever sabotaged a relationship/dating because you were afraid of getting married/commitment? If so, explain. Never sabotaged.
27. Are you afraid of getting married? If so, why or for what reason(s)? If not, why or for what reason? Not afraid. I go for what I want being a go-getter.
28. Have you been in a position where you were in a relationship or engaged to please others, even though, you knew in your heart that was not the right person for you? No.
29. Have you considered adopting a child(ren), foster care, or some other means, if you never give birth to any child(ren) of your own? If so, what option did you consider and why? None of the above.
30. Do you need healing or to come to terms with some pain(s) from the past before you can be open to getting married? Maybe.
31. Have you ever tried online dating to find a mate? If so, what was that experience like? Tinder once, just to check what happens there.
32. Looking back, would you do anything differently? If so, please explain. If not, please explain. I would have maybe engaged in a serious relationship in college maybe.
33. For those of you that want to get married, what qualities do you want in a spouse? Marriage is a big no.
34. Should a woman who is at least 40 years old, (who dates), be dating for the purpose of getting married? Yes.
35. How are you living your best life? Playing golf is my thing.

36. Name some accomplishments, goals, or visions you aspire to complete, have completed, or are working on. Representing my company in golf tournament and being the best.

37. Is there anything else you would like to say on this subject (being a woman who is at least 40 years old, have never been married before, with no children)? No.

1. Name: Victoria B.
2. Country: USA
3. City and/or State: New York
4. Are you happy/satisfied with being single? No.
5. Are you happy/satisfied with not having any children? Not happy/satisfied
6. Do you or have you ever envied other women who are married and have a child(ren)? No, I don't.
7. When you let others know that you have never been married and have no children, what was their response? What was your response to their response? "Marriage is not a bed of roses that is what some say. My response has always been the fact no one would love to be alone on a stormy night.
8. What have you learned about being single, with no kids? That being independent is good, but children are crucial for continuity.
9. What advice do you have for other women 40 and over, who have never been married and never had children? Work hard since nothing comes easily nowadays.
10. For those of you that don't ever want to get married or have children, have you encountered any negativity or criticism about this decision? Yes.
11. Do you have any regrets? No.
12. Do you choose to be single, with no kids, or is it circumstantial? Please explain. It is circumstantial. Our family has orphans whom we take care of.

13. Have you ever ruined or sabotaged an opportunity to get married/engaged, because of (fear of rejection, commitment, or another reason)? Yes.
14. If your answer is "Yes" above please explain. Fear of rejection by the guy I was dating since he was of a different faith. I feared being rejected by the guys family also, having quite a number of orphans I decided not to be.
15. Do you feel pressured to get married and have a family from outside sources (ex., family, church, friends, society, etc.)? No.
16. Have you ever felt embarrassed about being over 40 and never been married and no kids? Yes.
17. Have you had a conversation with God about your situation? Yes.
18. How do you feel about waiting on God to send you the right husband? God who listens in silence will answer in silence. Though I don't feel like it is a priority.
19. Do you believe you would have already been married by now? Why? How? Yes, I believe.
20. Are you okay if you never get married and have children? Do you accept this? Are you content? Why? Somehow.
21. What advice or words of wisdom would you give to other women in general (whether single or not, with kids or not)? To never taste alcohol, it is the surest route to failure.
22. Have you ever been tempted to get married or have a child because you got tired of waiting and you felt time was running out? Give examples. No.
23. Have you been engaged or thought you were going to get married and realized it was going to be a big mistake? What happened? Yes, being a Christian myself and the guy being of a different faith, I felt it was a big mistake.
24. Give examples of how you respond to people who question you as to why you're not married? I tell them am happy and that is all.
25. Have you ever thought about what it would be like to be married with children? It would have reminded me of my childhood.

26. Have you ever sabotaged a relationship/dating because you were afraid of getting married/commitment? If so, explain. Yes, I was once dating a narcissist who I refused to get married to.

27. Are you afraid of getting married? If so, why or for what reason(s)? If not, why or for what reason? Yes, I am afraid of marrying because I feel it is too late now.

28. Have you been in a position where you were in a relationship or engaged to please others, even though, you knew in your heart that was not the right person for you? Yes.

29. Have you considered adopting a child(ren), foster care, or some other means, if you never give birth to any child(ren) of your own? If so, what option did you consider and why? No. I am already doing foster care.

30. Do you need healing or to come to terms with some pain(s) from the past before you can be open to getting married? No.

31. Have you ever tried online dating to find a mate? If so, what was that experience like? Yes, and it was amazing.

32. Looking back, would you do anything differently? If so, please explain. If not, please explain. No, I believe I have no control of my past.

33. For those of you that want to get married, what qualities do you want in a spouse? I don't want to.

34. Should a woman who is at least 40 years old, (who dates), be dating for the purpose of getting married? No.

35. How are you living your best life? I love traveling.

36. Name some accomplishments, goals, or visions you aspire to complete, have completed, or are working on. I am currently working on my body weight.

37. Is there anything else you would like to say on this subject (being a woman who is at least 40 years old, have never been married before, with no children)? No.

1. Name: Babette Q.
2. Country: USA
3. City and/or State: Virginia
4. Are you happy/satisfied with being single? No.
5. Are you happy/satisfied with not having any children? Not happy/satisfied.
6. Do you or have you ever envied other women who are married and have a child(ren)? Sometimes I do.
7. When you let others know that you have never been married and have no children, what was their response? What was your response to their response? I don't care what they say.
8. What have you learned about being single, with no kids? I have learned that I might grow old alone without someone to take care of me.
9. What advice do you have for other women 40 and over, who have never been married and never had children? If they have an opportunity, they should grab it since being single is a lonely lifestyle.
10. For those of you that don't ever want to get married or have children, have you encountered any negativity or criticism about this decision? Yes
11. Do you have any regrets? No.
12. Do you choose to be single, with no kids, or is it circumstantial? Please explain. It was circumstantial due to financial reasons I choose to since marriage is expensive.
13. Have you ever ruined or sabotaged an opportunity to get married/engaged, because of (fear of rejection, commitment, or another reason)? Yes.
14. If your answer is "Yes" above please explain. Financial reasons.
15. Do you feel pressured to get married and have a family from outside sources (ex., family, church, friends, society, etc.)? Yes.

16. Have you ever felt embarrassed about being over 40 and never been married and no kids? Yes.
17. Have you had a conversation with God about your situation? Yes.
18. How do you feel about waiting on God to send you the right husband? I believe God will finally send.
19. Do you believe you would have already been married by now? Why? How? No.
20. Are you okay if you never get married and have children? Do you accept this? Are you content? Why? Yes, Okay if I achieve my life goals.
21. What advice or words of wisdom would you give to other women in general (whether single or not, with kids or not)? To grind hard.
22. Have you ever been tempted to get married or have a child because you got tired of waiting and you felt time was running out? Give examples. No.
23. Have you been engaged or thought you were going to get married and realized it was going to be a big mistake? What happened? Yes. The guy did not align with my financial goals.
24. Give examples of how you respond to people who question you as to why you're not married? I tell them to mind their own business and half of their problems will be solved.
25. Have you ever thought about what it would be like to be married with children? I know it is nice but not at the expense of my life goals.
26. Have you ever sabotaged a relationship/dating because you were afraid of getting married/commitment? If so, explain. No.
27. Are you afraid of getting married? If so, why or for what reason(s)? If not, why or for what reason? Not afraid.
28. Have you been in a position where you were in a relationship or engaged to please others, even though, you knew in your heart that was not the right person for you? No.
29. Have you considered adopting a child(ren), foster care, or some other means, if you never give birth to any child(ren) of

your own? If so, what option did you consider and why? Foster care.

30. Do you need healing or to come to terms with some pain(s) from the past before you can be open to getting married? No.

31. Have you ever tried online dating to find a mate? If so, what was that experience like? Once...good experience.

32. Looking back, would you do anything differently? If so, please explain. If not, please explain. Balance between finances and family.

33. For those of you that want to get married, what qualities do you want in a spouse? Financial independence.

34. Should a woman who is at least 40 years old, (who dates), be dating for the purpose of getting married? No.

35. How are you living your best life? Making money.

36. Name some accomplishments, goals, or visions you aspire to complete, have completed, or are working on. Becoming a millionaire in my 30's.

37. Is there anything else you would like to say on this subject (being a woman who is at least 40 years old, have never been married before, with no children)? I just want to congratulate you for the book!

1. Name: Avery D.
2. Country: USA
3. City and/or State: Denver
4. Are you happy/satisfied with being single? Yes.
5. Are you happy/satisfied with not having any children? Yes, I am happy/satisfied.
6. Do you or have you ever envied other women who are married and have a child(ren)? No, I don't.
7. When you let others know that you have never been married and have no children, what was their response? What was your response to their response? I normally tell them I have preference for nonmonogamy.
8. What have you learned about being single, with no kids? It is fun.
9. What advice do you have for other women 40 and over, who have never been married and never had children? To have fun, enjoy life. You gotta live once.
10. For those of you that don't ever want to get married or have children, have you encountered any negativity or criticism about this decision? No.
11. Do you have any regrets? No.
12. Do you choose to be single, with no kids, or is it circumstantial? Please explain. I choose to. I have preference for nonmonogamy.
13. Have you ever ruined or sabotaged an opportunity to get married/engaged, because of (fear of rejection, commitment, or another reason)? No.
14. If your answer is "Yes" above please explain. Not applicable.
15. Do you feel pressured to get married and have a family from outside sources (ex., family, church, friends, society, etc.)? No.
16. Have you ever felt embarrassed about being over 40 and never been married and no kids? Yes.

17. Have you had a conversation with God about your situation? Yes.

18. How do you feel about waiting on God to send you the right husband? I believe in destiny.

19. Do you believe you would have already been married by now? Why? How? Yes, if I had to settle would have long ago.

20. Are you okay if you never get married and have children? Do you accept this? Are you content? Why? Yes, I am okay.

21. What advice or words of wisdom would you give to other women in general (whether single or not, with kids or not)? To work hard and actualize their dreams. Their success is not tied to a man.

22. Have you ever been tempted to get married or have a child because you got tired of waiting and you felt time was running out? Give examples. No.

23. Have you been engaged or thought you were going to get married and realized it was going to be a big mistake? What happened? Not yet.

24. Give examples of how you respond to people who question you as to why you're not married? Why care?

25. Have you ever thought about what it would be like to be married with children? I normally think it will be hectic balancing between career and family.

26. Have you ever sabotaged a relationship/dating because you were afraid of getting married/commitment? If so, explain. Not yet.

27. Are you afraid of getting married? If so, why or for what reason(s)? If not, why or for what reason? I am afraid of marrying the wrong person who will claim what I genuinely worked hard for to be his.

28. Have you been in a position where you were in a relationship or engaged to please others, even though, you knew in your heart that was not the right person for you? Yes.

29. Have you considered adopting a child(ren), foster care, or some other means, if you never give birth to any child(ren) of

your own? If so, what option did you consider and why? Foster care.

30. Do you need healing or to come to terms with some pain(s) from the past before you can be open to getting married? No.

31. Have you ever tried online dating to find a mate? If so, what was that experience like? Severally, it was a great experience.

32. Looking back, would you do anything differently? If so, please explain. If not, please explain. I believe there is nothing I did bad in the past.

33. For those of you that want to get married, what qualities do you want in a spouse? Wealthy, neat, and sharp upstairs.

34. Should a woman who is at least 40 years old, (who dates), be dating for the purpose of getting married? Yes.

35. How are you living your best life? Making profits and traveling the world.

36. Name some accomplishments, goals, or visions you aspire to complete, have completed, or are working on. I finally went for a trip I have been longing for at Serengeti and Masaai Mara in Kenya.

37. Is there anything else you would like to say on this subject (being a woman who is at least 40 years old, have never been married before with no children? To stand by their principle. Live your life.

1. Name: Di P.
2. Country: US
3. City and/or State: Austin, TX
4. Are you happy/satisfied with being single? Maybe.
5. Are you happy/satisfied with not having any children? Not happy/satisfied.
6. Do you or have you ever envied other women who are married and have a child(ren)? Yes.

7. When you let others know that you have never been married and have no children, what was their response? What was your response to their response? They are surprised. Some encourage more to have Faith. I appreciate those who show concern.
8. What have you learned about being single, with no kids? I have learned that life is meaningless without a family.
9. What advice do you have for other women 40 and over, who have never been married and never had children? Never give up.
10. For those of you that don't ever want to get married or have children, have you encountered any negativity or criticism about this decision? No.
11. Do you have any regrets? Yes.
12. Do you choose to be single, with no kids, or is it circumstantial? Please explain. My choice.
13. Have you ever ruined or sabotaged an opportunity to get married/engaged, because of (fear of rejection, commitment, or another reason)? Yes.
14. If your answer is "Yes" above please explain. My parents forced me to get married to a person older than me. I ran away.
15. Do you feel pressured to get married and have a family from outside sources (ex., family, church, friends, society, etc.)? Yes.
16. Have you ever felt embarrassed about being over 40 and never been married and no kids? Yes.
17. Have you had a conversation with God about your situation? Yes.
18. How do you feel about waiting on God to send you the right husband? I believe God is faithful and He will ultimately send me the right person at the right time.
19. Do you believe you would have already been married by now? Why? How? I believe God's timing is the best for me.
20. Are you okay if you never get married and have children? Do you accept this? Are you content? Why? No okay.
21. What advice or words of wisdom would you give to other women in general (whether single or not, with kids or not)? Children are a blessing from God.

22. Have you ever been tempted to get married or have a child because you got tired of waiting and you felt time was running out? Give examples. Yes, severally.
23. Have you been engaged or thought you were going to get married and realized it was going to be a big mistake? What happened? Yes, being married off to an old man.
24. Give examples of how you respond to people who question you as to why you're not married? Why bother?
25. Have you ever thought about what it would be like to be married with children? It comes to my mind many times.
26. Have you ever sabotaged a relationship/dating because you were afraid of getting married/commitment? If so, explain. Yes, with my ex-boyfriend since my parents did not approve the relationship, I was afraid then, Unfortunately, I still feel he was the right person for me.
27. Are you afraid of getting married? If so, why or for what reason(s)? If not, why or for what reason? For now, I am not afraid.
28. Have you been in a position where you were in a relationship or engaged to please others, even though, you knew in your heart that was not the right person for you? Yes.
29. Have you considered adopting a child(ren), foster care, or some other means, if you never give birth to any child(ren) of your own? If so, what option did you consider and why? Foster care.
30. Do you need healing or to come to terms with some pain(s) from the past before you can be open to getting married? Yes.
31. Have you ever tried online dating to find a mate? If so, what was that experience like? Several times. Many sites today are full of millennials who are not the type I am looking for.
32. Looking back, would you do anything differently? If so, please explain. If not, please explain. I would have taken charge of my life in my twenties to avoid being unmarried by 40.
33. For those of you that want to get married, what qualities do you want in a spouse? Listening, good looks, and prayerful.

34. Should a woman who is at least 40 years old, (who dates), be dating for the purpose of getting married? No.
35. How are you living your best life? I eat well, exercise, and focus on my career.
36. Name some accomplishments, goals, or visions you aspire to complete, have completed, or are working on. I am working on Startup dealing with Desktop Virtualization and hope to expand globally in 5-10 years' time.
37. Is there anything else you would like to say on this subject (being a woman who is at least 40 years old, have never been married before, with no children)? Do not judge a book by its cover. You never know the reasons.

1. Name: Luna S.
2. Country: US
3. City and/or State: Alaska
4. Are you happy/satisfied with being single? Yes.
5. Are you happy/satisfied with not having any children? Yes, I am happy/satisfied.
6. Do you or have you ever envied other women who are married and have a child(ren)? No.
7. When you let others know that you have never been married and have no children, what was their response? What was your response to their response? They normally laugh and some make jokes at me, but I laugh, sarcastically too.
8. What have you learned about being single, with no kids? It doesn't matter.
9. What advice do you have for other women 40 and over, who have never been married and never had children? You can live a successful life without being married or not having children.

10. For those of you that don't ever want to get married or have children, have you encountered any negativity or criticism about this decision? No.
11. Do you have any regrets? No.
12. Do you choose to be single, with no kids, or is it circumstantial? Please explain. I choose to be.
13. Have you ever ruined or sabotaged an opportunity to get married/engaged, because of (fear of rejection, commitment, or another reason)? Yes.
14. If your answer is "Yes" above please explain. I believe marriage is to help each other grow and not just for children production.
15. Do you feel pressured to get married and have a family from outside sources (ex., family, church, friends, society, etc.)? No.
16. Have you ever felt embarrassed about being over 40 and never been married and no kids? Yes.
17. Have you had a conversation with God about your situation? Yes.
18. How do you feel about waiting on God to send you the right husband? God wants us to put Him first, not a spouse. I'll tell you from experience, that it is possible to be happy with God and no spouse. I prayed to God many times after my last relationship a couple of years ago to help me to put Him first because I knew a spouse would never make me happy without Him being the center of my life. (After many failed relationships, I finally figured it out.) Not to say I don't want a spouse, but if God never gives me one that's okay. He has big plans for me that I am focused on right now.
19. Do you believe you would have already been married by now? Why? How? No. The primary purpose is always to help others. Not to have sex and make babies.
20. Are you okay if you never get married and have children? Do you accept this? Are you content? Why? Much okay.
21. What advice or words of wisdom would you give to other women in general (whether single or not, with kids or not)? Whatever you want it to be. You could define your life by having a great career. Or by traveling a lot. Or fixing up a cool car. You

could learn how to cook or mix drinks. You could learn another language. Your life is literally an open highway. There's far more to it than the traditional nuclear family. Some people believe there's only one way to live life. They're wrong. The sky is the limit unless you become an astronaut.

22. Have you ever been tempted to get married or have a child because you got tired of waiting and you felt time was running out? Give examples. Yes, many of us have our lives mapped out and are holding onto some idea of the point at which we'd like to be married, start a family, or score a corner office. Guidelines are nice but deciding to get engaged primarily because a certain year is approaching on the calendar is making a move out of fear. If you're motivated to get married mainly by the desire to avoid falling off track, or by some antiquated notion of being "washed up" after a certain age, you're not truly owning your decision, and likely not assessing the costs and benefits—not to mention the true attributes your potential spouse brings to the table for the long haul.

23. Have you been engaged or thought you were going to get married and realized it was going to be a big mistake? What happened? To fall in love with yourself, and to discover all the things that make you, you! To realize that you are way worth the effort of going out of your way to make you happy! I just spent most of my life trying so hard to make someone happy all the while he was using me to his fullest advantage and had no care or worry about the pain he caused me until he didn't have me anymore. Then I realized how many years I wasted on him when I could have been working on me.

24. Give examples of how you respond to people who question you as to why you're not married? Why do you ask?

25. Have you ever thought about what it would be like to be married with children? Marriage and children are just an outdated way of keeping you from having a life.

26. Have you ever sabotaged a relationship/dating because you were afraid of getting married/commitment? If so, explain. No.

27. Are you afraid of getting married? If so, why or for what reason(s)? If not, why or for what reason? Yes, I am afraid because I am used to my independent lifestyle. I do not want another person to interfere with it.

28. Have you been in a position where you were in a relationship or engaged to please others, even though, you knew in your heart that was not the right person for you? No.

29. Have you considered adopting a child(ren), foster care, or some other means, if you never give birth to any child(ren) of your own? If so, what option did you consider and why? Adoption is something on my list.

30. Do you need healing or to come to terms with some pain(s) from the past before you can be open to getting married? No.

31. Have you ever tried online dating to find a mate? If so, what was that experience like? Not yet.

32. Looking back, would you do anything differently? If so, please explain. If not, please explain. I would have interacted or socialized more and established quality connections.

33. For those of you that want to get married, what qualities do you want in a spouse? Someone I can trust and someone faithful.

34. Should a woman who is at least 40 years old, (who dates), be dating for the purpose of getting married? No.

35. How are you living your best life? In the end, our time on earth is limited and gone in a blink of an eye. I don't think we should care what others think of us, especially whether we are single or have kids. It's a waste of precious time.

36. Name some accomplishments, goals, or visions you aspire to complete, have completed, or are working on. My career goal is to be a Senior Manager, or I want to earn $60,000 while working in a Senior Managerial position.

37. Is there anything else you would like to say on this subject (being a woman who is at least 40 years old, have never been married before, with no children)? The meaning of life really comes down to the individual and what they value.

1. Name: Cammie K.
2. Country: USA
3. City and/or State: Georgia
4. Are you happy/satisfied with being single? No.
5. Are you happy/satisfied with not having any children? Not happy/satisfied.
6. Do you or have you ever envied other women who are married and have a child(ren)? Yes, I do.
7. When you let others know that you have never been married and have no children, what was their response? What was your response to their response? Most people are usually surprised and ask how come a beautiful woman like me is not married. I smile.
8. What have you learned about being single, with no kids? It is a boring life.
9. What advice do you have for other women 40 and over, who have never been married and never had children? I advise them to stay calm, patient, and pray to God.
10. For those of you that don't ever want to get married or have children, have you encountered any negativity or criticism about this decision? Yes.
11. Do you have any regrets? No.
12. Do you choose to be single, with no kids, or is it circumstantial? Please explain. It is circumstantial. I am barren.
13. Have you ever ruined or sabotaged an opportunity to get married/engaged, because of (fear of rejection, commitment, or another reason)? No.
14. If your answer is "Yes" above please explain. N/A
15. Do you feel pressured to get married and have a family from outside sources (ex., family, church, friends, society, etc.)? Yes.
16. Have you ever felt embarrassed about being over 40 and never been married and no kids? (This question was not answered).

17. Have you had a conversation with God about your situation? Yes.

18. How do you feel about waiting on God to send you the right husband? I normally feel bad because in reality, I know even if God gives me a husband, I will not be able to satisfy him as I cannot give him children.

19. Do you believe you would have already been married by now? Why? How? Yes. I believe if I wasn't a barren woman I would have already been married by now.

20. Are you okay if you never get married and have children? Do you accept this? Are you content? Why? I am not okay. I accept this since it is beyond my control that I am a barren woman.

21. What advice or words of wisdom would you give to other women in general (whether single or not, with kids or not)? Women should not judge other women who do not have children or are not married.

22. Have you ever been tempted to get married or have a child because you got tired of waiting and you felt time was running out? Give examples. I have been, but it pains. I have nothing I can do.

23. Have you been engaged or thought you were going to get married and realized it was going to be a big mistake? What happened? Yes, I have been engaged to a guy whom I loved so much, but when he realized I was barren, he left for good. It really pains me.

24. Give examples of how you respond to people who question you as to why you're not married? I normally feel bad. It is very painful. Especially being questioned by people who do not know anything about my situation. Most of the time, I tell them to be considerate.

25. Have you ever thought about what it would be like to be married with children? I know it would have been fun, I think often.

26. Have you ever sabotaged a relationship/dating because you were afraid of getting married/commitment? If so, explain. No.

27. Are you afraid of getting married? If so, why or for what reason(s)? If not, why or for what reason? I am afraid because even if I do my situation won't allow.
28. Have you been in a position where you were in a relationship or engaged to please others, even though, you knew in your heart that was not the right person for you? Yes.
29. Have you considered adopting a child(ren), foster care, or some other means, if you never give birth to any child(ren) of your own? If so, what option did you consider and why? I have considered caring for children of my relatives.
30. Do you need healing or to come to terms with some pain(s) from the past before you can be opened to getting married? No.
31. Have you ever tried online dating to find a mate? If so, what was that experience like? Never.
32. Looking back, would you do anything differently? If so, please explain. If not, please explain. I would have found an understanding partner. Explained my situation and allowed him to have a child with another woman, who we could have raised as my own.
33. For those of you that want to get married, what qualities do you want in a spouse? Understanding, loving, and God fearing.
34. Should a woman who is at least 40 years old, (who dates), be dating for the purpose of getting married? No.
35. How are you living your best life? I spend most of my time with women in my similar situation with whom we engage and grow together.
36. Name some accomplishments, goals, or visions you aspire to complete, have completed, or are working on. I aspire to be a medical doctor and currently, I am doing my PhD thesis.
37. Is there anything else you would like to say on this subject (being a woman who is at least 40 years old, have never been married before, with no children)? I would like to say it is not easy. Take charge and enjoy life that is what matters.

1. Name: Emma V.
2. Country: USA
3. City and/or State: Texas
4. Are you happy/satisfied with being single? Yes.
5. Are you happy/satisfied with not having any children? Not happy/satisfied.
6. Do you or have you ever envied other women who are married and have a child(ren)? Not at all.
7. When you let others know that you have never been married and have no children, what was their response? What was your response to their response? Most of them tell me to get married. I normally respond and tell them I will.
8. What have you learned about being single, with no kids? Most of them tell me to get married. It is so lonely.
9. What advice do you have for other women 40 and over, who have never been married and never had children? I would advise them not to overthink of their situation.
10. For those of you that don't ever want to get married or have children, have you encountered any negativity or criticism about this decision? Yes.
11. Do you have any regrets? Yes.
12. Do you choose to be single, with no kids, or is it circumstantial? Please explain. I choose to be single with no kids.
13. Have you ever ruined or sabotaged an opportunity to get married/engaged, because of (fear of rejection, commitment, or another reason)? Yes.
14. If your answer is "Yes" above please explain. I have been too busy with my business and one time when I was about to get married. I saw it as a distractor.
15. Do you feel pressured to get married and have a family from outside sources (ex., family, church, friends, society, etc.)? No.

16. Have you ever felt embarrassed about being over 40 and never been married and no kids? Yes.
17. Have you had a conversation with God about your situation? Yes.
18. How do you feel about waiting on God to send you the right husband? I am patient.
19. Do you believe you would have already been married by now? Why? How? Yes. If I wanted a husband, I have had many potential suitors, but they are not my type.
20. Are you okay if you never get married and have children? Do you accept this? Are you content? Why? I will be okay provided I have achieved my goals career wise.
21. What advice or words of wisdom would you give to other women in general (whether single or not, with kids or not)? I would advise my fellow women never to settle for less.
22. Have you ever been tempted to get married or have a child because you got tired of waiting and you felt time was running out? Give examples. I have never reached that point.
23. Have you been engaged or thought you were going to get married and realized it was going to be a big mistake? What happened? I was once engaged and called it quits because I was still busy building my business from scratch.
24. Give examples of how you respond to people who question you as to why you're not married? To me it is a non-issue and do not care about the opinions of other people.
25. Have you ever thought about what it would be like to be married with children? Yes, much of attention will be on my children.
26. Have you ever sabotaged a relationship/dating because you were afraid of getting married/commitment? If so, explain. Yes, I have sabotaged in order to focus on my business.
27. Are you afraid of getting married? If so, why or for what reason(s)? If not, why or for what reason? For now, I am not afraid of getting married. I believe I have what it takes, or I am mature enough to drive marriage life the way I want it to be.

28. Have you been in a position where you were in a relationship or engaged to please others, even though, you knew in your heart that was not the right person for you? Yes.

29. Have you considered adopting a child(ren), foster care, or some other means, if you never give birth to any child(ren) of your own? If so, what option did you consider and why? I prefer foster care as I see it more human.

30. Do you need healing or to come to terms with some pain(s) from the past before you can be open to getting married? No.

31. Have you ever tried online dating to find a mate? If so, what was that experience like? Yes, I have tried online dating sites for hook up and to satisfy my sexual needs, but not for long-term relationship that will lead to marriage. It has been successful.

32. Looking back, would you do anything differently? If so, please explain. If not, please explain. Looking back, I think I would have had children in my twenties so that by the time I am in my 40's they are old enough to help me with my business.

33. For those of you that want to get married, what qualities do you want in a spouse? I want a humble person who is respectful.

34. Should a woman who is at least 40 years old, (who dates), be dating for the purpose of getting married? Yes.

35. How are you living your best life? I spend most of my time in my business. It is my life and it's my everything.

36. Name some accomplishments, goals, or visions you aspire to complete, have completed, or are working on. I have managed to establish a five-star hotel for myself. To me it is a great achievement.

37. Is there anything else you would like to say on this subject (being a woman who is at least 40 years old, have never been married before, with no children)? For now, No.

1. Name: Ava Z.
2. Country: UK (United Kingdom)
3. City and/or State: London
4. Are you happy/satisfied with being single? Yes.
5. Are you happy/satisfied with not having any children? Yes, I am happy/satisfied.
6. Do you or have you ever envied other women who are married and have a child(ren)? Never.
7. When you let others know that you have never been married and have no children, what was their response? What was your response to their response? My friends tell me stories of their husbands and how they have disagreements and few talk about good times. I counter and tell them I have disagreements with no one since I am usually all alone.
8. What have you learned about being single, with no kids? I have learned that being single and no kids you have enough time to grow.
9. What advice do you have for other women 40 and over, who have never been married and never had children? Not to overthink too much about it.
10. For those of you that don't ever want to get married or have children, have you encountered any negativity or criticism about this decision? Yes.
11. Do you have any regrets? No.
12. Do you choose to be single, with no kids, or is it circumstantial? Please explain. I choose to be single.
13. Have you ever ruined or sabotaged an opportunity to get married/engaged, because of (fear of rejection, commitment, or another reason)? No.
14. If your answer is "Yes" above please explain. No.
15. Do you feel pressured to get married and have a family from outside sources (ex., family, church, friends, society, etc.)? No.

16. Have you ever felt embarrassed about being over 40 and never been married and no kids? Yes.
17. Have you had a conversation with God about your situation? No.
18. How do you feel about waiting on God to send you the right husband? Not waiting.
19. Do you believe you would have already been married by now? Why? How? No, I don't believe so.
20. Are you okay if you never get married and have children? Do you accept this? Are you content? Why? Yes, I do accept.
21. What advice or words of wisdom would you give to other women in general (whether single or not, with kids or not)? To always make decisions that will benefit them now and for the future.
22. Have you ever been tempted to get married or have a child because you got tired of waiting and you felt time was running out? Give examples. No.
23. Have you been engaged or thought you were going to get married and realized it was going to be a big mistake? What happened? No.
24. Give examples of how you respond to people who question you as to why you're not married? "I am not getting married anytime soon".
25. Have you ever thought about what it would be like to be married with children? I normally understand I wouldn't even have time for myself.
26. Have you ever sabotaged a relationship/dating because you were afraid of getting married/commitment? If so, explain. No.
27. Are you afraid of getting married? If so, why or for what reason(s)? If not, why or for what reason? Yes, I am afraid of sacrificing my career, dreams, and achievement to someone else.
28. Have you been in a position where you were in a relationship or engaged to please others, even though, you knew in your heart that was not the right person for you? Yes.
29. Have you considered adopting a child(ren), foster care, or some other means, if you never give birth to any child(ren) of

your own? If so, what option did you consider and why? Neither of the above.

30. Do you need healing or to come to terms with some pain(s) from the past before you can be open to getting married? No.

31. Have you ever tried online dating to find a mate? If so, what was that experience like? Not a fan and I haven't tried.

32. Looking back, would you do anything differently? If so, please explain. If not, please explain. I believe I made better choices in my past that I can do again.

33. For those of you that want to get married, what qualities do you want in a spouse? Not me.

34. Should a woman who is at least 40 years old, (who dates), be dating for the purpose of getting married? No.

35. How are you living your best life? Socializing and learning from the best, in order to improve myself.

36. Name some accomplishments, goals, or visions you aspire to complete, have completed, or are working on. I recently finished building myself the house of my dreams.

37. Is there anything else you would like to say on this subject (being a woman who is at least 40 years old, have never been married before, with no children)? (No answer to this question).

1. Name: Elizabeth B.
2. Country: USA
3. City and/or State: Nebraska
4. Are you happy/satisfied with being single? No.
5. Are you happy/satisfied with not having any children? Not happy/satisfied.
6. Do you or have you ever envied other women who are married and have a child(ren)? I don't envy. I love.
7. When you let others know that you have never been married and have no children, what was their response? What was your response to their response? Majority are usually remorseful, but I reply by telling them I am okay.
8. What have you learned about being single, with no kids? I have learned that kids are a blessing.
9. What advice do you have for other women 40 and over, who have never been married and never had children? Not to rush to find a spouse for the purpose of pleasing the society.
10. For those of you that don't ever want to get married or have children, have you encountered any negativity or criticism about this decision? No.
11. Do you have any regrets? No.
12. Do you choose to be single, with no kids, or is it circumstantial? Please explain. Circumstantial, I have not had luck in relationships.
13. Have you ever ruined or sabotaged an opportunity to get married/engaged, because of (fear of rejection, commitment, or another reason)? No.
14. If your answer is "Yes" above please explain. N/A
15. Do you feel pressured to get married and have a family from outside sources (ex., family, church, friends, society, etc.)? Yes.
16. Have you ever felt embarrassed about being over 40 and never been married and no kids? Yes.

17. Have you had a conversation with God about your situation? Yes.
18. How do you feel about waiting on God to send you the right husband? I
feel everything happens for a reason.
19. Do you believe you would have already been married by now? Why? How? Yes, I believe if I found the right person.
20. Are you okay if you never get married and have children? Do you accept this? Are you content? Why? I wouldn't be okay what if I died who will take care of my kids.
21. What advice or words of wisdom would you give to other women in general (whether single or not, with kids or not)? Never to fall in love with a married man.
22. Have you ever been tempted to get married or have a child because you got tired of waiting and you felt time was running out? Give examples. My friends used to put pressure on me until I told them clearly that if they do not understand me then they are not even my friends in the first place.
23. Have you been engaged or thought you were going to get married and realized it was going to be a big mistake? What happened? I was engaged but for this it wasn't a mistake. My partner travelled to a distant country, and we couldn't manage the long-distance relationship.
24. Give examples of how you respond to people who question you as to why you're not married? Honestly, I don't respond.
25. Have you ever thought about what it would be like to be married with children? I admire children a lot. I think I would have created lifetime bond with my children.
26. Have you ever sabotaged a relationship/dating because you were afraid of getting married/commitment? If so, explain. Yes. Long distance commitment.
27. Are you afraid of getting married? If so, why or for what reason(s)? If not, why or for what reason? I am not afraid, in fact, I am looking forward to the day.

28. Have you been in a position where you were in a relationship or engaged to please others, even though, you knew in your heart that was not the right person for you? Yes.

29. Have you considered adopting a child(ren), foster care, or some other means, if you never give birth to any child(ren) of your own? If so, what option did you consider and why? Adoption.

30. Do you need healing or to come to terms with some pain(s) from the past before you can be opened to getting married? No.

31. Have you ever tried online dating to find a mate? If so, what was that experience like? Have tried several, but never met a serious person-majority are after sex.

32. Looking back, would you do anything differently? If so, please explain. If not, please explain. Went to more weddings, functions just maybe I could have been married long ago.

33. For those of you that want to get married, what qualities do you want in a spouse? 5 years older than me and sober in mind, faithful, loving, I know it is too much to ask.

34. Should a woman who is at least 40 years old, (who dates), be dating for the purpose of getting married? Yes.

35. How are you living your best life? I go to the gym a lot.

36. Name some accomplishments, goals, or visions you aspire to complete, have completed, or are working on. I am working on YouTube scripts.

37. Is there anything else you would like to say on this subject (being a woman who is at least 40 years old, have never been married before, with no children)? We deserve love too.

1. Name: Scarlett T.
2. Country: USA
3. City and/or State: North Carolina
4. Are you happy/satisfied with being single? No.

5. Are you happy/satisfied with not having any children? Not happy/satisfied.
6. Do you or have you ever envied other women who are married and have a child(ren)? I am not the envious type.
7. When you let others know that you have never been married and have no children, what was their response? What was your response to their response? I don't let people know in the first place.
8. What have you learned about being single, with no kids? Companionship is good.
9. What advice do you have for other women 40 and over, who have never been married and never had children? Avoid dating apps. The last thing a dating app wants you to do is meet someone, because when you meet someone, you stop giving it money. This is a very basic concept that single women "looking for love" overlook almost universally. Dating apps are incentivized to keep you single and swiping for as long as they possible can.
10. For those of you that don't ever want to get married or have children, have you encountered any negativity or criticism about this decision? Yes.
11. Do you have any regrets? No.
12. Do you choose to be single, with no kids, or is it circumstantial? Please explain. I choose.
13. Have you ever ruined or sabotaged an opportunity to get married/engaged, because of (fear of rejection, commitment, or another reason)? Yes.
14. If your answer is "Yes" above please explain. Yes, I forced a scenario that I can't mention here just to have the relationship end.
15. Do you feel pressured to get married and have a family from outside sources (ex., family, church, friends, society, etc.)? Yes.
16. Have you ever felt embarrassed about being over 40 and never been married and no kids? Maybe.
17. Have you had a conversation with God about your situation? Maybe.

18. How do you feel about waiting on God to send you the right husband? God is the one that gives and also takes.
19. Do you believe you would have already been married by now? Why? How? I don't believe if I would, I would have been.
20. Are you okay if you never get married and have children? Do you accept this? Are you content? Why? I will accept the outcome.
21. What advice or words of wisdom would you give to other women in general (whether single or not, with kids or not)? You can't pour from an empty cup.
22. Have you ever been tempted to get married or have a child because you got tired of waiting and you felt time was running out? Give examples. I normally feel the pressure myself.
23. Have you been engaged or thought you were going to get married and realized it was going to be a big mistake? What happened? Not yet.
24. Give examples of how you respond to people who question you as to why you're not married? Top focus on their lives.
25. Have you ever thought about what it would be like to be married with children? No.
26. Have you ever sabotaged a relationship/dating because you were afraid of getting married/commitment? If so, explain. Not Yet.
27. Are you afraid of getting married? If so, why or for what reason(s)? If not, why or for what reason? Not afraid.
28. Have you been in a position where you were in a relationship or engaged to please others, even though, you knew in your heart that was not the right person for you? No.
29. Have you considered adopting a child(ren), foster care, or some other means, if you never give birth to any child(ren) of your own? If so, what option did you consider and why? Adoption if fine.
30. Do you need healing or to come to terms with some pain(s) from the past before you can be open to getting married? No.
31. Have you ever tried online dating to find a mate? If so, what was that experience like? Never.

32. Looking back, would you do anything differently? If so, please explain. If not, please explain. Nothing, I can change.
33. For those of you that want to get married, what qualities do you want in a spouse? Caring.
34. Should a woman who is at least 40 years old, (who dates), be dating for the purpose of getting married? No.
35. How are you living your best life? Traveling a lot.
36. Name some accomplishments, goals, or visions you aspire to complete, have completed, or are working on. Finish my degree.
37. Is there anything else you would like to say on this subject (being a woman who is at least 40 years old, have never been married before, with no children)? No.

1. Name: Grace R.
2. Country: USA
3. City and/or State: Texas
4. Are you happy/satisfied with being single? Yes.
5. Are you happy/satisfied with not having any children? Yes, I am happy/satisfied.
6. Do you or have you ever envied other women who are married and have a child(ren)? No.
7. When you let others know that you have never been married and have no children, what was their response? What was your response to their response? No response.
8. What have you learned about being single, with no kids? That I can enjoy life.
9. What advice do you have for other women 40 and over, who have never been married and never had children? To focus on their careers.
10. For those of you that don't ever want to get married or have children, have you encountered any negativity or criticism about this decision? No.

11. Do you have any regrets? No.
12. Do you choose to be single, with no kids, or is it circumstantial? Please explain. Circumstances.
13. Have you ever ruined or sabotaged an opportunity to get married/engaged, because of (fear of rejection, commitment, or another reason)? No.
14. If your answer is "Yes" above please explain. N/A
15. Do you feel pressured to get married and have a family from outside sources (ex., family, church, friends, society, etc.)? No.
16. Have you ever felt embarrassed about being over 40 and never been married and no kids? No.
17. Have you had a conversation with God about your situation? No.
18. How do you feel about waiting on God to send you the right husband? N/A
19. Do you believe you would have already been married by now? Why? How? No.
20. Are you okay if you never get married and have children? Do you accept this? Are you content? Why? Okay.
21. What advice or words of wisdom would you give to other women in general (whether single or not, with kids or not)? Life is short.
22. Have you ever been tempted to get married or have a child because you got tired of waiting and you felt time was running out? Give examples. No.
23. Have you been engaged or thought you were going to get married and realized it was going to be a big mistake? What happened? No.
24. Give examples of how you respond to people who question you as to why you're not married? Ignore.
25. Have you ever thought about what it would be like to be married with children? No.
26. Have you ever sabotaged a relationship/dating because you were afraid of getting married/commitment? If so, explain. No.
27. Are you afraid of getting married? If so, why or for what reason(s)? If not, why or for what reason? No.

28. Have you been in a position where you were in a relationship or engaged to please others, even though, you knew in your heart that was not the right person for you? Yes.

29. Have you considered adopting a child(ren), foster care, or some other means, if you never give birth to any child(ren) of your own? If so, what option did you consider and why? Adopting.

30. Do you need healing or to come to terms with some pain(s) from the past before you can be open to getting married? No.

31. Have you ever tried online dating to find a mate? If so, what was that experience like? No.

32. Looking back, would you do anything differently? If so, please explain. If not, please explain. No.

33. For those of you that want to get married, what qualities do you want in a spouse? Not.

34. Should a woman who is at least 40 years old, (who dates), be dating for the purpose of getting married? No.

35. How are you living your best life? Taking care of my body.

36. Name some accomplishments, goals, or visions you aspire to complete, have completed, or are working on. (No answer).

37. Is there anything else you would like to say on this subject (being a woman who is at least 40 years old, have never been married before, with no children)? Nothing.

1. Name: Ellie G.
2. Country: USA
3. City and/or State: Chicago
4. Are you happy/satisfied with being single? No.
5. Are you happy/satisfied with not having any children? Not happy/satisfied.
6. Do you or have you ever envied other women who are married and have a child(ren)? No, I have never envied.
7. When you let others know that you have never been married and have no children, what was their response? What was your response to their response? To avoid the many questions, I do not bring up the topic unless asked to.
8. What have you learned about being single, with no kids? That those women with kids should be thankful to God.
9. What advice do you have for other women 40 and over, who have never been married and never had children? Not to lose hope.
10. For those of you that don't ever want to get married or have children, have you encountered any negativity or criticism about this decision? No.
11. Do you have any regrets? No.
12. Do you choose to be single, with no kids, or is it circumstantial? Please explain. I did not choose. Circumstances forced me.
13. Have you ever ruined or sabotaged an opportunity to get married/engaged, because of (fear of rejection, commitment, or another reason)? No.
14. If your answer is "Yes" above please explain. N/A
15. Do you feel pressured to get married and have a family from outside sources (ex., family, church, friends, society, etc.)? No.
16. Have you ever felt embarrassed about being over 40 and never been married and no kids? No.

17. Have you had a conversation with God about your situation? No.
18. How do you feel about waiting on God to send you the right husband? God has every reason for each person on Earth.
19. Do you believe you would have already been married by now? Why? How? No.
20. Are you okay if you never get married and have children? Do you accept this? Are you content? Why? I am not okay.
21. What advice or words of wisdom would you give to other women in general (whether single or not, with kids or not)? To make themselves proud.
22. Have you ever been tempted to get married or have a child because you got tired of waiting and you felt time was running out? Give examples. Yes.
23. Have you been engaged or thought you were going to get married and realized it was going to be a big mistake? What happened? No.
24. Give examples of how you respond to people who question you as to why you're not married? To leave me alone.
25. Have you ever thought about what it would be like to be married with children? It is painful thinking about.
26. Have you ever sabotaged a relationship/dating because you were afraid of getting married/commitment? If so, explain. No.
27. Are you afraid of getting married? If so, why or for what reason(s)? If not, why or for what reason? Not afraid.
28. Have you been in a position where you were in a relationship or engaged to please others, even though, you knew in your heart that was not the right person for you? No.
29. Have you considered adopting a child(ren), foster care, or some other means, if you never give birth to any child(ren) of your own? If so, what option did you consider and why? Foster.
30. Do you need healing or to come to terms with some pain(s) from the past before you can be open to getting married? No.
31. Have you ever tried online dating to find a mate? If so, what was that experience like? Never.

32. Looking back, would you do anything differently? If so, please explain. If not, please explain. Dated in my 20's.
33. For those of you that want to get married, what qualities do you want in a spouse? Hardworking.
34. Should a woman who is at least 40 years old, (who dates), be dating for the purpose of getting married? No.
35. How are you living your best life? Traveling.
36. Name some accomplishments, goals, or visions you aspire to complete, have completed, or are working on. Best mixologist.
37. Is there anything else you would like to say on this subject (being a woman who is at least 40 years old, have never been married before, with no children)? Women in this category should form a forum.

1. Name: Nora K.
2. Country: USA
3. City and/or State: Illinois
4. Are you happy/satisfied with being single? No.
5. Are you happy/satisfied with not having any children? Not happy/satisfied.
6. Do you or have you ever envied other women who are married and have a child(ren)? Never.
7. When you let others know that you have never been married and have no children, what was their response? What was your response to their response? They ask about the experience, and I give them honest opinion.
8. What have you learned about being single, with no kids? It is unhealthy.
9. What advice do you have for other women 40 and over, who have never been married and never had children? Remain steadfast and have faith.

10. For those of you that don't ever want to get married or have children, have you encountered any negativity or criticism about this decision? No.

11. Do you have any regrets? No answer.

12. Do you choose to be single, with no kids, or is it circumstantial? Please explain. I choose to.

13. Have you ever ruined or sabotaged an opportunity to get married/engaged, because of (fear of rejection, commitment, or another reason)? No.

14. If your answer is "Yes" above please explain. No.

15. Do you feel pressured to get married and have a family from outside sources (ex., family, church, friends, society, etc.)? No.

16. Have you ever felt embarrassed about being over 40 and never been married and no kids? No.

17. Have you had a conversation with God about your situation? No.

18. How do you feel about waiting on God to send you the right husband? N/A

19. Do you believe you would have already been married by now? Why? How? No.

20. Are you okay if you never get married and have children? Do you accept this? Are you content? Why? Not okay.

21. What advice or words of wisdom would you give to other women in general (whether single or not, with kids or not)? To maintain their purity.

22. Have you ever been tempted to get married or have a child because you got tired of waiting and you felt time was running out? Give examples. No.

23. Have you been engaged or thought you were going to get married and realized it was going to be a big mistake? What happened? No.

24. Give examples of how you respond to people who question you as to why you're not married? Ignore them.

25. Have you ever thought about what it would be like to be married with children? No.

26. Have you ever sabotaged a relationship/dating because you were afraid of getting married/commitment? If so, explain. No.

27. Are you afraid of getting married? If so, why or for what reason(s)? If not, why or for what reason? Not afraid.

28. Have you been in a position where you were in a relationship or engaged to please others, even though, you knew in your heart that was not the right person for you? Yes.

29. Have you considered adopting a child(ren), foster care, or some other means, if you never give birth to any child(ren) of your own? If so, what option did you consider and why? Adoption.

30. Do you need healing or to come to terms with some pain(s) from the past before you can be open to getting married? No.

31. Have you ever tried online dating to find a mate? If so, what was that experience like? Not yet but thinking about it.

32. Looking back, would you do anything differently? If so, please explain. If not, please explain. I focus on future not the things I cannot change.

33. For those of you that want to get married, what qualities do you want in a spouse? Loving.

34. Should a woman who is at least 40 years old, (who dates), be dating for the purpose of getting married? Yes.

35. How are you living your best life? Music.

36. Name some accomplishments, goals, or visions you aspire to complete, have completed, or are working on. Working on my music album.

37. Is there anything else you would like to say on this subject (being a woman who is at least 40 years old, have never been married before, with no children)? No.

1. Name: Violet M.
2. Country: USA
3. City and/or State: Oklahoma
4. Are you happy/satisfied with being single? No.
5. Are you happy/satisfied with not having any children? Not happy/satisfied.
6. Do you or have you ever envied other women who are married and have a child(ren)? No.
7. When you let others know that you have never been married and have no children, what was their response? What was your response to their response? They normally want to know the reasons as to why I am still single, and I normally respond.
8. What have you learned about being single, with no kids? Boring.
9. What advice do you have for other women 40 and over, who have never been married and never had children? To choose what will make them happy and go for it.
10. For those of you that don't ever want to get married or have children, have you encountered any negativity or criticism about this decision? No.
11. Do you have any regrets? No.
12. Do you choose to be single, with no kids, or is it circumstantial? Please explain. I choose too, though I want kids, but I don't need a serious relationship that will lead to marriage.
13. Have you ever ruined or sabotaged an opportunity to get married/engaged, because of (fear of rejection, commitment, or another reason)? No.
14. If your answer is "Yes" above please explain. No.
15. Do you feel pressured to get married and have a family from outside sources (ex., family, church, friends, society, etc.)? No.
16. Have you ever felt embarrassed about being over 40 and never been married and no kids? No.

17. Have you had a conversation with God about your situation? No.
18. How do you feel about waiting on God to send you the right husband? I feel God will find someone who we are really compatible with when the right time comes.
19. Do you believe you would have already been married by now? Why? How? Yes, I do have belief, but I had not yet met a compatible person yet.
20. Are you okay if you never get married and have children? Do you accept this? Are you content? Why? Not content.
21. What advice or words of wisdom would you give to other women in general (whether single or not, with kids or not)? Women should have their own life.
22. Have you ever been tempted to get married or have a child because you got tired of waiting and you felt time was running out? Give examples. Never.
23. Have you been engaged or thought you were going to get married and realized it was going to be a big mistake? What happened? No.
24. Give examples of how you respond to people who question you as to why you're not married? I normally tell them that I just got out of a long-term relationship.
25. Have you ever thought about what it would be like to be married with children? Not really.
26. Have you ever sabotaged a relationship/dating because you were afraid of getting married/commitment? If so, explain. I have not sabotaged any.
27. Are you afraid of getting married? If so, why or for what reason(s)? If not, why or for what reason? Not afraid but if I find a compatible person why not.
28. Have you been in a position where you were in a relationship or engaged to please others, even though, you knew in your heart that was not the right person for you? Yes.
29. Have you considered adopting a child(ren), foster care, or some other means, if you never give birth to any child(ren) of

your own? If so, what option did you consider and why? Foster care.

30. Do you need healing or to come to terms with some pain(s) from the past before you can be open to getting married? Yes.

31. Have you ever tried online dating to find a mate? If so, what was that experience like? Not before.

32. Looking back, would you do anything differently? If so, please explain. If not, please explain. Past is gone. I don't concentrate on bitter memories or past.

33. For those of you that want to get married, what qualities do you want in a spouse? Unwavering love and good communication.

34. Should a woman who is at least 40 years old, (who dates), be dating for the purpose of getting married? No.

35. How are you living your best life? Socializing and hanging out often.

36. Name some accomplishments, goals, or visions you aspire to complete, have completed, or are working on. Finish my master's degree before 45.

37. Is there anything else you would like to say on this subject (being a woman who is at least 40 years old, have never been married before, with no children)? Marry a partner who will cheer you up.

1. Name: Everly P.
2. Country: USA
3. City and/or State: Wisconsin
4. Are you happy/satisfied with being single? Yes.
5. Are you happy/satisfied with not having any children? Yes, I am happy/satisfied.
6. Do you or have you ever envied other women who are married and have a child(ren)? Never.
7. When you let others know that you have never been married and have no children, what was their response? What was your response to their response? I don't tell other people, only friends.
8. What have you learned about being single, with no kids? It is enjoyable.
9. What advice do you have for other women 40 and over, who have never been married and never had children? There is time for everything.
10. For those of you that don't ever want to get married or have children, have you encountered any negativity or criticism about this decision? No.
11. Do you have any regrets? No.
12. Do you choose to be single, with no kids, or is it circumstantial? Please explain. Having been raised by abusive parents, I choose to remain this way.
13. Have you ever ruined or sabotaged an opportunity to get married/engaged, because of (fear of rejection, commitment, or another reason)? No.
14. If your answer is "Yes" above please explain. No.
15. Do you feel pressured to get married and have a family from outside sources (ex., family, church, friends, society, etc.)? Yes.
16. Have you ever felt embarrassed about being over 40 and never been married and no kids? Yes.

17. Have you had a conversation with God about your situation? Yes.
18. How do you feel about waiting on God to send you the right husband? God is a wonderful God. He cares.
19. Do you believe you would have already been married by now? Why? How? No, I choose to live this way.
20. Are you okay if you never get married and have children? Do you accept this? Are you content? Why? I am okay.
21. What advice or words of wisdom would you give to other women in general (whether single or not, with kids or not)? Those married, to take care of their husbands.
22. Have you ever been tempted to get married or have a child because you got tired of waiting and you felt time was running out? Give examples. No.
23. Have you been engaged or thought you were going to get married and realized it was going to be a big mistake? What happened? No.
24. Give examples of how you respond to people who question you as to why you're not married? Ignore the question.
25. Have you ever thought about what it would be like to be married with children? I reflect back to a nuclear family set up full of noise.
26. Have you ever sabotaged a relationship/dating because you were afraid of getting married/commitment? If so, explain. No.
27. Are you afraid of getting married? If so, why or for what reason(s)? If not, why or for what reason? Yes, I am afraid. I am used to my own space.
28. Have you been in a position where you were in a relationship or engaged to please others, even though, you knew in your heart that was not the right person for you? No.
29. Have you considered adopting a child(ren), foster care, or some other means, if you never give birth to any child(ren) of your own? If so, what option did you consider and why? Adopting or foster care all are great choices.
30. Do you need healing or to come to terms with some pain(s) from the past before you can be open to getting married? Maybe.

31. Have you ever tried online dating to find a mate? If so, what was that experience like? No.
32. Looking back, would you do anything differently? If so, please explain. If not, please explain. No.
33. For those of you that want to get married, what qualities do you want in a spouse? (No answer).
34. Should a woman who is at least 40 years old, (who dates), be dating for the purpose of getting married? No.
35. How are you living your best life? Partying and having fun.
36. Name some accomplishments, goals, or visions you aspire to complete, have completed, or are working on. I aspire to visit Space.
37. Is there anything else you would like to say on this subject (being a woman who is at least 40 years old, have never been married before, with no children)? No.

1. Name: Paisley O.
2. Country: USA
3. City and/or State: Hawaii
4. Are you happy/satisfied with being single? No.
5. Are you happy/satisfied with not having any children? Not happy/satisfied.
6. Do you or have you ever envied other women who are married and have a child(ren)? No.
7. When you let others know that you have never been married and have no children, what was their response? What was your response to their response? I normally appreciate those that stand with me and not bother those that do not.
8. What have you learned about being single, with no kids? The importance of kids and a spouse.

9. What advice do you have for other women 40 and over, who have never been married and never had children? I would advise them never to lose hope.
10. For those of you that don't ever want to get married or have children, have you encountered any negativity or criticism about this decision? (No answer).
11. Do you have any regrets? No.
12. Do you choose to be single, with no kids, or is it circumstantial? Please explain. Single by choice (personal reasons).
13. Have you ever ruined or sabotaged an opportunity to get married/engaged, because of (fear of rejection, commitment, or another reason)? No.
14. If your answer is "Yes" above please explain. No.
15. Do you feel pressured to get married and have a family from outside sources (ex., family, church, friends, society, etc.)? No.
16. Have you ever felt embarrassed about being over 40 and never been married and no kids? No.
17. Have you had a conversation with God about your situation? Maybe.
18. How do you feel about waiting on God to send you the right husband? God is understanding and I believe my time will come.
19. Do you believe you would have already been married by now? Why? How? No, because I never took my past relationships seriously.
20. Are you okay if you never get married and have children? Do you accept this? Are you content? Why? Not okay to be sincere.
21. What advice or words of wisdom would you give to other women in general (whether single or not, with kids or not)? To work and make money and leave a better legacy for prosperity.
22. Have you ever been tempted to get married or have a child because you got tired of waiting and you felt time was running out? Give examples. Never.
23. Have you been engaged or thought you were going to get married and realized it was going to be a big mistake? What happened? Yes, I was engaged but unfortunately my parents were the ones who thought it was a big mistake not me.

24. Give examples of how you respond to people who question you as to why you're not married? I normally tell them not to mind, God is in control.

25. Have you ever thought about what it would be like to be married with children? Wonderful! Yes, quite a lot to be honest.

26. Have you ever sabotaged a relationship/dating because you were afraid of getting married/commitment? If so, explain. Yes, I sabotaged my first relationship because I was afraid maybe I was too young to get married.

27. Are you afraid of getting married? If so, why or for what reason(s)? If not, why or for what reason? For now, I am not afraid. I believe I have experienced a lot.

28. Have you been in a position where you were in a relationship or engaged to please others, even though, you knew in your heart that was not the right person for you? No.

29. Have you considered adopting a child(ren), foster care, or some other means, if you never give birth to any child(ren) of your own? If so, what option did you consider and why? I have considered adopting quite a lot.

30. Do you need healing or to come to terms with some pain(s) from the past before you can be open to getting married? No.

31. Have you ever tried online dating to find a mate? If so, what was that experience like? Yes Tinder, once though.

32. Looking back, would you do anything differently? If so, please explain. If not, please explain. I wouldn't have sabotaged my first relationship.

33. For those of you that want to get married, what qualities do you want in a spouse? Loving and obedience. Above all the fear of God.

34. Should a woman who is at least 40 years old, (who dates), be dating for the purpose of getting married? No.

35. How are you living your best life? Church going.

36. Name some accomplishments, goals, or visions you aspire to complete, have completed, or are working on. Best hockey player.

37. Is there anything else you would like to say on this subject (being a woman who is at least 40 years old, have never been married before, with no children)? Not now.

1. Name: Limbani D.
2. Country: USA
3. City and/or State: Louisiana
4. Are you happy/satisfied with being single? Yes.
5. Are you happy/satisfied with not having any children? Yes, I am happy/satisfied.
6. Do you or have you ever envied other women who are married and have child(ren)? No.
7. When you let others know that you have never been married and have no children, what was their response? What was your response to their response? No Response.
8. What have you learned about being single, with no kids? I have learned to be content in Jesus Christ according to I Corinthians 7:32. I love being single. I can skip the middleman and go straight to God. He is my everything.
9. What advice do you have for other women 40 and over, who have never been married and never had children? (No answer).
10. For those of you that don't ever want to get married or have children, have you encountered any negativity or criticism about this decision? No.
11. Do you have any regrets? No.
12. Do you choose to be single, with no kids, or is it circumstantial? Please explain. (No answer).
13. Have you ever ruined or sabotaged an opportunity to get married/engaged, because of (fear of rejection, commitment, or another reason)? No.
14. If your answer is "Yes" above please explain. N/A

15. Do you feel pressured to get married and have a family from outside sources (ex., family, church, friends, society, etc.)? No.

16. Have you ever felt embarrassed about being over 40 and never been married and no kids? No.

17. Have you had a conversation with God about your situation? No.

18. How do you feel about waiting on God to send you the right husband? I don't want to get married. I'm content with Jesus.

19. Do you believe you would have already been married by now? Why? How? No.

20. Are you okay if you never get married and have children? Do you accept this? Are you content? Why? Yes, because of Jesus.

21. What advice or words of wisdom would you give to other women in general (whether single or not, with kids or not)? Be a Proverbs 31 Woman.

22. Have you ever been tempted to get married or have a child because you got tired of waiting and you felt time was running out? Give examples. No and Double No.

23. Have you been engaged or thought you were going to get married and realized it was going to be a big mistake? What happened? No.

24. Give examples of how you respond to people who question you as to why you're not married? I was never asked why.

25. Have you ever thought about what it would be like to be married with children? No.

26. Have you ever sabotaged a relationship/dating because you were afraid of getting married/commitment? If so, explain. No.

27. Are you afraid of getting married? If so, why or for what reason(s)? If not, why or for what reason? No.

28. Have you been in a position where you were in a relationship or engaged to please others, even though, you knew in your heart that was not the right person for you? No.

29. Have you considered adopting a child(ren), foster care, or some other means, if you never give birth to any child(ren) of your own? If so, what option did you consider and why? No.

30. Do you need healing or to come to terms with some pain(s) from the past before you can be open to getting married? No.

31. Have you ever tried online dating to find a mate? If so, what was that experience like? No.

32. Looking back, would you do anything differently? If so, please explain. If not, please explain. No, because I believe my life is already planned out by God.

33. For those of you that want to get married, what qualities do you want in a spouse? N/A

34. Should a woman who is at least 40 years old, (who dates), be dating for the purpose of getting married? No.

35. How are you living your best life? By being a Christian.

36. Name some accomplishments, goals, or visions you aspire to complete, have completed, or are working on. The only vision I have is to live for Jesus in this world and to live with him throughout eternity.

37. Is there anything else you would like to say on this subject (being a woman who is at least 40 years old, have never been married before, with no children)? Fall in love with Jesus. He will never leave you or forsake you. But if you want to get married, let God choose your mate, like he chose Rebecca for Isaac in Genesis 24:12-15.

1. Name: Natalie B.
2. Country: USA
3. City and/or State: Dallas
4. Are you happy/satisfied with being single? Yes.
5. Are you happy/satisfied with not having any children? Yes, I am happy/satisfied.
6. Do you or have you ever envied other women who are married and have a child(ren)? Sometimes I wish I was like them.

7. When you let others know that you have never been married and have no children, what was their response? What was your response to their response? They tease me and I feel offended sometimes leaving the table where respect is no longer being served.
8. What have you learned about being single, with no kids? Self-control is very important.
9. What advice do you have for other women 40 and over, who have never been married and never had children? Be patient, they will have kids soon.
10. For those of you that don't ever want to get married or have children, have you encountered any negativity or criticism about this decision? No.
11. Do you have any regrets? No.
12. Do you choose to be single, with no kids, or is it circumstantial? Please explain. Circumstantial.
13. Have you ever ruined or sabotaged an opportunity to get married/engaged, because of (fear of rejection, commitment, or another reason)? No.
14. If your answer is "Yes" above please explain. No.
15. Do you feel pressured to get married and have a family from outside sources (ex., family, church, friends, society, etc.)? No.
16. Have you ever felt embarrassed about being over 40 and never been married and no kids? Maybe.
17. Have you had a conversation with God about your situation? (No answer).
18. How do you feel about waiting on God to send you the right husband? I haven't had a conversation with God about the right husband.
19. Do you believe you would have already been married by now? Why? How? Yes, if I grabbed the available opportunities.
20. Are you okay if you never get married and have children? Do you accept this? Are you content? Why? I wouldn't be okay.
21. What advice or words of wisdom would you give to other women in general (whether single or not, with kids or not)? They should stand tall and not let anyone take advantage of them.

22. Have you ever been tempted to get married or have a child because you got tired of waiting and you felt time was running out? Give examples. Yes, when I was in my 30's, I used to worry about menopause often.
23. Have you been engaged or thought you were going to get married and realized it was going to be a big mistake? What happened? No.
24. Give examples of how you respond to people who question you as to why you're not married? I try to be frank as possible with them and tell them I can't give birth.
25. Have you ever thought about what it would be like to be married with children? No.
26. Have you ever sabotaged a relationship/dating because you were afraid of getting married/commitment? If so, explain. No.
27. Are you afraid of getting married? If so, why or for what reason(s)? If not, why or for what reason? No, I am not.
28. Have you been in a position where you were in a relationship or engaged to please others, even though, you knew in your heart that was not the right person for you? Maybe.
29. Have you considered adopting a child(ren), foster care, or some other means, if you never give birth to any child(ren) of your own? If so, what option did you consider and why? Adoption.
30. Do you need healing or to come to terms with some pain(s) from the past before you can be open to getting married? No.
31. Have you ever tried online dating to find a mate? If so, what was that experience like? Yes, back in college and it was fun meeting random people.
32. Looking back, would you do anything differently? If so, please explain. If not, please explain. I would focus more on traveling to different places.
33. For those of you that want to get married, what qualities do you want in a spouse? Truthful.
34. Should a woman who is at least 40 years old, (who dates), be dating for the purpose of getting married? No.
35. How are you living your best life? Currently I am working in an orphanage, and it gives me so much joy.

36. Name some accomplishments, goals, or visions you aspire to complete, have completed, or are working on. Starting my orphanage.

37. Is there anything else you would like to say on this subject (being a woman who is at least 40 years old, have never been married before, with no children)? No.

1. Name: Elena E.
2. Country: USA
3. City and/or State: Wyoming
4. Are you happy/satisfied with being single? No.
5. Are you happy/satisfied with not having any children? Not happy/satisfied.
6. Do you or have you ever envied other women who are married and have a child(ren)? Yes.
7. When you let others know that you have never been married and have no children, what was their response? What was your response to their response? (No answer).
8. What have you learned about being single, with no kids? That one should focus on his or her own life.
9. What advice do you have for other women 40 and over, who have never been married and never had children? They should be patient.
10. For those of you that don't ever want to get married or have children, have you encountered any negativity or criticism about this decision? No.
11. Do you have any regrets? No.
12. Do you choose to be single, with no kids, or is it circumstantial? Please explain. It is circumstantial since I am not able to give birth.

13. Have you ever ruined or sabotaged an opportunity to get married/engaged, because of (fear of rejection, commitment, or another reason)? No.

14. If your answer is "Yes" above please explain. No.

15. Do you feel pressured to get married and have a family from outside sources (ex., family, church, friends, society, etc.)? (No answer).

16. Have you ever felt embarrassed about being over 40 and never been married and no kids? Yes.

17. Have you had a conversation with God about your situation? No.

18. How do you feel about waiting on God to send you the right husband? I feel God will do so definitely.

19. Do you believe you would have already been married by now? Why? How? No, I don't believe so.

20. Are you okay if you never get married and have children? Do you accept this? Are you content? Why? Of course, I will not be okay.

21. What advice or words of wisdom would you give to other women in general (whether single or not, with kids or not)? Your bills give it to God. Your career, give it to God. Your life, give it to God.

22. Have you ever been tempted to get married or have a child because you got tired of waiting and you felt time was running out? Give examples. Yes, it was a temptation, but fortunately I was able to control it.

23. Have you been engaged or thought you were going to get married and realized it was going to be a big mistake? What happened? Never.

24. Give examples of how you respond to people who question you as to why you're not married? My life, my rules, and my choice.

25. Have you ever thought about what it would be like to be married with children? Yes, love wins, I mean an atmosphere full of love.

26. Have you ever sabotaged a relationship/dating because you were afraid of getting married/commitment? If so, explain. No.

27. Are you afraid of getting married? If so, why or for what reason(s)? If not, why or for what reason? Yes, I am afraid. I have had previous negative experiences regarding marriage and the memories scare me.

28. Have you been in a position where you were in a relationship or engaged to please others, even though, you knew in your heart that was not the right person for you? No.

29. Have you considered adopting a child(ren), foster care, or some other means, if you never give birth to any child(ren) of your own? If so, what option did you consider and why? Foster care.

30. Do you need healing or to come to terms with some pain(s) from the past before you can be open to getting married? No.

31. Have you ever tried online dating to find a mate? If so, what was that experience like? Bumble was a good experience.

32. Looking back, would you do anything differently? If so, please explain. If not, please explain. Yes, I could perhaps take advantage of online dating sites to the best of my advantage. I feel that I did not quite explore them enough.

33. For those of you that want to get married, what qualities do you want in a spouse? Maturity (ex. Emotional).

34. Should a woman who is at least 40 years old, (who dates), be dating for the purpose of getting married? No.

35. How are you living your best life? Currently, I am focusing on my financial goals so as to be able to actualize my dreams.

36. Name some accomplishments, goals, or visions you aspire to complete, have completed, or are working on. I organized a successful charity event.

37. Is there anything else you would like to say on this subject (being a woman who is at least 40 years old, have never been married before, with no children)? I would just tell my fellow women in this category not to lower their standards and settle for less.

1. Name: Claire R.
2. Country: USA
3. City and/or State: Kansas
4. Are you happy/satisfied with being single? Yes.
5. Are you happy/satisfied with not having any children? Yes, I am happy/satisfied.
6. Do you or have you ever envied other women who are married and have a child(ren)? No, I don't like children.
7. When you let others know that you have never been married and have no children, what was their response? What was your response to their response? My friends always joke that they will look for me a spouse, but we normally end up cracking jokes instead.
8. What have you learned about being single, with no kids? I have learned that one can choose to live life the way they want.
9. What advice do you have for other women 40 and over, who have never been married and never had children? Their breakthrough is coming. They should trust the process.
10. For those of you that don't ever want to get married or have children, have you encountered any negativity or criticism about this decision? No.
11. Do you have any regrets? No.
12. Do you choose to be single, with no kids, or is it circumstantial? Please explain. I choose to be single.
13. Have you ever ruined or sabotaged an opportunity to get married/engaged, because of (fear of rejection, commitment, or another reason)? No.
14. If your answer is "Yes" above please explain. No.
15. Do you feel pressured to get married and have a family from outside sources (ex., family, church, friends, society, etc.)? Maybe.
16. Have you ever felt embarrassed about being over 40 and never been married and no kids? No.

17. Have you had a conversation with God about your situation? No.
18. How do you feel about waiting on God to send you the right husband? Not me.
19. Do you believe you would have already been married by now? Why? How? Yes, if I wanted, I could already have finalized long ago.
20. Are you okay if you never get married and have children? Do you accept this? Are you content? Why? Yes, I am content, I don't know if this feeling will ever change.
21. What advice or words of wisdom would you give to other women in general (whether single or not, with kids or not)? Women should not marry a man hoping he will change.
22. Have you ever been tempted to get married or have a child because you got tired of waiting and you felt time was running out? Give examples. Never.
23. Have you been engaged or thought you were going to get married and realized it was going to be a big mistake? What happened? Yes, once the guy I was dating was a narcissist and I thought taking the relationship to the next stage with such a person would be risky.
24. Give examples of how you respond to people who question you as to why you're not married? I ask them if they are married themselves or not?
25. Have you ever thought about what it would be like to be married with children? Never.
26. Have you ever sabotaged a relationship/dating because you were afraid of getting married/commitment? If so, explain. Yes, once the guy I was dating was a narcissist and I though taking the relationship to the next stage with such a person would be risky.
27. Are you afraid of getting married? If so, why or for what reason(s)? If not, why or for what reason? I am not afraid. I have made a decision not to.
28. Have you been in a position where you were in a relationship or engaged to please others, even though, you knew in your heart that was not the right person for you? Yes.

29. Have you considered adopting a child(ren), foster care, or some other means, if you never give birth to any child(ren) of your own? If so, what option did you consider and why? (No answer).

30. Do you need healing or to come to terms with some pain(s) from the past before you can be open to getting married? No.

31. Have you ever tried online dating to find a mate? If so, what was that experience like? Not tried any yet.

32. Looking back, would you do anything differently? If so, please explain. If not, please explain. Looking back, I don't have any regrets.

33. For those of you that want to get married, what qualities do you want in a spouse? Not me.

34. Should a woman who is at least 40 years old, (who dates), be dating for the purpose of getting married? Yes.

35. How are you living your best life? I am being just the best version of myself and not being a version of someone else.

36. Name some accomplishments, goals, or visions you aspire to complete, have completed, or are working on. I am a great long-distance runner.

37. Is there anything else you would like to say on this subject (being a woman who is at least 40 years old, have never been married before, with no children)? No.

1. Name: Ivy C.
2. Country: USA
3. City and/or State: Texas
4. Are you happy/satisfied with being single? No.
5. Are you happy/satisfied with not having any children? Not happy/satisfied.
6. Do you or have you ever envied other women who are married and have a child(ren)? No, I believe in applauding others before my time comes.
7. When you let others know that you have never been married and have no children, what was their response? What was your response to their response? Most are normally surprised and do not believe so.
8. What have you learned about being single, with no kids? I have learned that as much as one may enjoy being single, kids are also necessary for the future.
9. What advice do you have for other women 40 and over, who have never been married and never had children? Not to despair.
10. For those of you that don't ever want to get married or have children, have you encountered any negativity or criticism about this decision? No.
11. Do you have any regrets? Yes.
12. Do you choose to be single, with no kids, or is it circumstantial? Please explain. It is circumstantial, I haven't been lucky.
13. Have you ever ruined or sabotaged an opportunity to get married/engaged, because of (fear of rejection, commitment, or another reason)? No.
14. If your answer is "Yes" above please explain. N/A
15. Do you feel pressured to get married and have a family from outside sources (ex., family, church, friends, society, etc.)? No.
16. Have you ever felt embarrassed about being over 40 and never been married and no kids? No.

17. Have you had a conversation with God about your situation? Yes.
18. How do you feel about waiting on God to send you the right husband? I believe God will finally do His part.
19. Do you believe you would have already been married by now? Why? How? Yes, if luck was on my side, then why not.
20. Are you okay if you never get married and have children? Do you accept this? Are you content? Why? Not okay.
21. What advice or words of wisdom would you give to other women in general (whether single or not, with kids or not)? I would advise those with kids not to judge those without.
22. Have you ever been tempted to get married or have a child because you got tired of waiting and you felt time was running out? Give examples. Never before.
23. Have you been engaged or thought you were going to get married and realized it was going to be a big mistake? What happened? No.
24. Give examples of how you respond to people who question you as to why you're not married? I tell them not to be worried. I will invite them soon to my wedding.
25. Have you ever thought about what it would be like to be married with children? Awesome experience.
26. Have you ever sabotaged a relationship/dating because you were afraid of getting married/commitment? If so, explain. I haven't sabotaged any. I am always careful before committing.
27. Are you afraid of getting married? If so, why or for what reason(s)? If not, why or for what reason? I am not afraid of marriage, in fact, I have been longing for one but with the right person.
28. Have you been in a position where you were in a relationship or engaged to please others, even though, you knew in your heart that was not the right person for you? Yes.
29. Have you considered adopting a child(ren), foster care, or some other means, if you never give birth to any child(ren) of your own? If so, what option did you consider and why? Foster Care.

30. Do you need healing or to come to terms with some pain(s) from the past before you can be open to getting married? No.
31. Have you ever tried online dating to find a mate? If so, what was that experience like? Never.
32. Looking back, would you do anything differently? If so, please explain. If not, please explain. Perhaps, I would have a given online dating a try.
33. For those of you that want to get married, what qualities do you want in a spouse? I want a man who respect my opinions and listen to what I say.
34. Should a woman who is at least 40 years old, (who dates), be dating for the purpose of getting married? No.
35. How are you living your best life? Volunteering in charity organizations.
36. Name some accomplishments, goals, or visions you aspire to complete, have completed, or are working on. I have vision in being an effective leader and also eyeing political opportunities.
37. Is there anything else you would like to say on this subject (being a woman who is at least 40 years old, have never been married before, with no children)? It is never too old to have a child.

1. Name: Flossy Z.
2. Country: USA
3. City and/or State: Seattle
4. Are you happy/satisfied with being single? No.
5. Are you happy/satisfied with not having any children? Not happy/satisfied.
6. Do you or have you ever envied other women who are married and have a child(ren)? No. I was raised to celebrate the success of other people before my success.

7. When you let others know that you have never been married and have no children, what was their response? What was your response to their response? "Irreconcilable" differences were the cause. I do not necessary answer every question asked.
8. What have you learned about being single, with no kids? Kids make life worthwhile.
9. What advice do you have for other women 40 and over, who have never been married and never had children? Don't worry too much about being single.
10. For those of you that don't ever want to get married or have children, have you encountered any negativity or criticism about this decision? Maybe.
11. Do you have any regrets? No.
12. Do you choose to be single, with no kids, or is it circumstantial? Please explain. I choose to be.
13. Have you ever ruined or sabotaged an opportunity to get married/engaged, because of (fear of rejection, commitment, or another reason)? No.
14. If your answer is "Yes" above please explain. N/A
15. Do you feel pressured to get married and have a family from outside sources (ex., family, church, friends, society, etc.)? No.
16. Have you ever felt embarrassed about being over 40 and never been married and no kids? Yes.
17. Have you had a conversation with God about your situation? Yes.
18. How do you feel about waiting on God to send you the right husband? I pray more. Not a two-minute prayer but taking time to pray to God.
19. Do you believe you would have already been married by now? Why? How? Probably.
20. Are you okay if you never get married and have children? Do you accept this? Are you content? Why? To me marriage is a capstone that comes after I have achieved my goals. If I don't fine, then provided I have accomplished my other goals in life.
21. What advice or words of wisdom would you give to other women in general (whether single or not, with kids or not)? The

most important factor in a relationship is not communication, but respect.

22. Have you ever been tempted to get married or have a child because you got tired of waiting and you felt time was running out? Give examples. Yes, It felt like a desperation move rather than a marriage tied with love.

23. Have you been engaged or thought you were going to get married and realized it was going to be a big mistake? What happened? Was a chemistry issue. A lack of compatibility.

24. Give examples of how you respond to people who question you as to why you're not married? Focus on own family.

25. Have you ever thought about what it would be like to be married with children? Children change our lives. They make them a little more hectic and busy and complicated.

26. Have you ever sabotaged a relationship/dating because you were afraid of getting married/commitment? If so, explain. The prospect of marriage is overwhelmingly frightening to me. I think at the root of all this is the need to love myself. I think if you love yourself, you're better able to love someone else and not rely on their opinion of you to make you feel beautiful or wanted or lovely or enough. I sabotaged my past relationship because I felt I wasn't loved enough by my partner and really needed a break.

27. Are you afraid of getting married? If so, why or for what reason(s)? If not, why or for what reason? Yes, since according to research unmarried people are healthier compared to married people.

28. Have you been in a position where you were in a relationship or engaged to please others, even though, you knew in your heart that was not the right person for you? Yes.

29. Have you considered adopting a child(ren), foster care, or some other means, if you never give birth to any child(ren) of your own? If so, what option did you consider and why? Adopting.

30. Do you need healing or to come to terms with some pain(s) from the past before you can be open to getting married? No.

31. Have you ever tried online dating to find a mate? If so, what was that experience like? Online dating is rather shallow.

32. Looking back, would you do anything differently? If so, please explain. If not, please explain. Would not change anything, because your experiences have helped you grow.

33. For those of you that want to get married, what qualities do you want in a spouse? Honesty, and lives with integrity.

34. Should a woman who is at least 40 years old, (who dates), be dating for the purpose of getting married? No.

35. How are you living your best life? Appreciating what I have—simply because it's impossible to feel grateful and stressed at the same time and that's a powerful place to be.

36. Name some accomplishments, goals, or visions you aspire to complete, have completed, or are working on. Publish a novel.

37. Is there anything else you would like to say on this subject (being a woman who is at least 40 years old, have never been married before, with no children)? No matter what anyone ever tells you, staying in an abusive relationship is not safe. I chose safety, hope, and life.

1. Name: Ulrika X.
2. Country: USA
3. City and/or State: Austin, TX
4. Are you happy/satisfied with being single? Yes.
5. Are you happy/satisfied with not having any children? Yes, I am happy/satisfied.
6. Do you or have you ever envied other women who are married and have a child(ren)? No.
7. When you let others know that you have never been married and have no children, what was their response? What was your response to their response? Although I am used to vague responses to this scenario, it also depends on the situation or place and the person asking the question.

8. What have you learned about being single, with no kids? You can't get if it is not your turn.

9. What advice do you have for other women 40 and over, who have never been married and never had children? Marriage is not a bed of roses for lazy bones.

10. For those of you that don't ever want to get married or have children, have you encountered any negativity or criticism about this decision? No.

11. Do you have any regrets? Maybe.

12. Do you choose to be single, with no kids, or is it circumstantial? Please explain. Circumstantial as explained above.

13. Have you ever ruined or sabotaged an opportunity to get married/engaged, because of (fear of rejection, commitment, or another reason)? No.

14. If your answer is "Yes" above please explain. N/A

15. Do you feel pressured to get married and have a family from outside sources (ex., family, church, friends, society, etc.)? No.

16. Have you ever felt embarrassed about being over 40 and never been married and no kids? No.

17. Have you had a conversation with God about your situation? No.

18. How do you feel about waiting on God to send you the right husband? I believe God has three answers when you ask for something: NO, YES, and WAIT. Maybe God is telling me to wait and preparing something good.

19. Do you believe you would have already been married by now? Why? How? Yes, to some old guy who wanted me as a second wife, but I declined.

20. Are you okay if you never get married and have children? Do you accept this? Are you content? Why? Sure, if I can't control something I do not stress over it.

21. What advice or words of wisdom would you give to other women in general (whether single or not, with kids or not)? Never indulge in self-defeating thoughts.

22. Have you ever been tempted to get married or have a child because you got tired of waiting and you felt time was running

out? Give examples. Yes, in fact there was a time I was given a timeframe by my family to either choose between celibacy and marriage. I thought they were joking, but luckily, we navigated through.

23. Have you been engaged or thought you were going to get married and realized it was going to be a big mistake? What happened? I was engaged to someone who was nagging, and I felt it was a big mistake.

24. Give examples of how you respond to people who question you as to why you're not married? It is not a priority at the moment.

25. Have you ever thought about what it would be like to be married with children? Yes, I imagine I will have a solid emotional support system.

26. Have you ever sabotaged a relationship/dating because you were afraid of getting married/commitment? If so, explain. The only guy I ever loved felt constant insecurity about the relationship and end up making 20 calls to me in a day every day. I got tired.

27. Are you afraid of getting married? If so, why or for what reason(s)? If not, why or for what reason? I am not afraid. Marriage is not on my bucket list.

28. Have you been in a position where you were in a relationship or engaged to please others, even though, you knew in your heart that was not the right person for you? No.

29. Have you considered adopting a child(ren), foster care, or some other means, if you never give birth to any child(ren) of your own? If so, what option did you consider and why? Adopting.

30. Do you need healing or to come to terms with some pain(s) from the past before you can be open to getting married? No.

31. Have you ever tried online dating to find a mate? If so, what was that experience like? No.

32. Looking back, would you do anything differently? If so, please explain. If not, please explain. Let bygones be bygones, that has always been my policy.

33. For those of you that want to get married, what qualities do you want in a spouse? Has a sense of humor!

34. Should a woman who is at least 40 years old, (who dates), be dating for the purpose of getting married? No
35. How are you living your best life? Vacations, when I get time.
36. Name some accomplishments, goals, or visions you aspire to complete, have completed, or are working on. See all of the Seven Wonders of the World.
37. Is there anything else you would like to say on this subject (being a woman who is at least 40 years old, have never been married before, with no children)? Low self-esteem, negative self-talk, related negative emotions, which are further bolstered by subsequent failures in various realms of life can all lead to people behaving in ways that take them further away from their potential love. BE CAREFUL.

1. Name: Katherine M.
2. Country: USA
3. City and/or State: Washington
4. Are you happy/satisfied with being single? Maybe.
5. Are you happy/satisfied with not having any children? Not happy/satisfied.
6. Do you or have you ever envied other women who are married and have a child(ren)? Never.
7. When you let others know that you have never been married and have no children, what was their response? What was your response to their response? I tell them I'm the same person in a marriage that they see for themselves. Honest, open, loving, supportive, humorous, devoted, caring, empathetic. I overwhelmed the family therapist when she asked.
8. What have you learned about being single, with no kids? There's no time limit on experiences.

9. What advice do you have for other women 40 and over, who have never been married and never had children? (No answer given).
10. For those of you that don't ever want to get married or have children, have you encountered any negativity or criticism about this decision? No.
11. Do you have any regrets? Maybe.
12. Do you choose to be single, with no kids, or is it circumstantial? Please explain. Circumstantial.
13. Have you ever ruined or sabotaged an opportunity to get married/engaged, because of (fear of rejection, commitment, or another reason)? No.
14. If your answer is "Yes" above please explain. No.
15. Do you feel pressured to get married and have a family from outside sources (ex., family, church, friends, society, etc.)? No.
16. Have you ever felt embarrassed about being over 40 and never been married and no kids? No.
17. Have you had a conversation with God about your situation? Yes.
18. How do you feel about waiting on God to send you the right husband? Time will come.
19. Do you believe you would have already been married by now? Why? How? Yes, I believe so.
20. Are you okay if you never get married and have children? Do you accept this? Are you content? Why? Not okay.
21. What advice or words of wisdom would you give to other women in general (whether single or not, with kids or not)? To be 100% responsible of everything they do.
22. Have you ever been tempted to get married or have a child because you got tired of waiting and you felt time was running out? Give examples. No.
23. Have you been engaged or thought you were going to get married and realized it was going to be a big mistake? What happened? Yes, I was older than the guy I was dating, and I thought age was not just a number, but a factor in marriage.

24. Give examples of how you respond to people who question you as to why you're not married? It's a question I get a lot and I am sick of answering it. I do not answer it anymore because I cannot sacrifice my privacy to satisfy the curiosity of someone else.

25. Have you ever thought about what it would be like to be married with children? Yes, I know kids would greatly change my daily way of life.

26. Have you ever sabotaged a relationship/dating because you were afraid of getting married/commitment? If so, explain. Never.

27. Are you afraid of getting married? If so, why or for what reason(s)? If not, why or for what reason? Not afraid but it depends on the person you are getting married to.

28. Have you been in a position where you were in a relationship or engaged to please others, even though, you knew in your heart that was not the right person for you? Yes.

29. Have you considered adopting a child(ren), foster care, or some other means, if you never give birth to any child(ren) of your own? If so, what option did you consider and why? Foster care preferably.

30. Do you need healing or to come to terms with some pain(s) from the past before you can be open to getting married? No.

31. Have you ever tried online dating to find a mate? If so, what was that experience like? Yes, but you will not make the same level of connection like by old school dating.

32. Looking back, would you do anything differently? If so, please explain. If not, please explain. Fear, I'd get rid of it. I'd be able to say yes when my husband wants to go somewhere that requires us to drive places. I'd be able to smile and greet people without my stomach being twisted in knots.

33. For those of you that want to get married, what qualities do you want in a spouse? A spouse who is good in communication, easy to trust, and also physical attributes that are attractive.

34. Should a woman who is at least 40 years old, (who dates), be dating for the purpose of getting married? No.

35. How are you living your best life? Making intimacy with God the most important part of everyday. Drawing close to Jesus and staying there.

36. Name some accomplishments, goals, or visions you aspire to complete, have completed, or are working on. Master a musical instrument: Guitar.

37. Is there anything else you would like to say on this subject (being a woman who is at least 40 years old, have never been married before, with no children)? People should stop asking people why they are single and no children.

1. Name: Hannah G.
2. Country: USA
3. City and/or State: Idaho
4. Are you happy/satisfied with being single? Yes.
5. Are you happy/satisfied with not having any children? Yes, I am happy/satisfied.
6. Do you or have you ever envied other women who are married and have a child(ren)? Yes.
7. When you let others know that you have never been married and have no children, what was their response? What was your response to their response? To get married, time is running out. I tell them to hold their horses tight.
8. What have you learned about being single, with no kids? I have learned the importance of having friends.
9. What advice do you have for other women 40 and over, who have never been married and never had children? I would advise them their marital status is not to prevent us from having the best shot at life.
10. For those of you that don't ever want to get married or have children, have you encountered any negativity or criticism about this decision? Yes.

11. Do you have any regrets? Maybe.
12. Do you choose to be single, with no kids, or is it circumstantial? Please explain. I choose to be single with no kids because I was raised in a violent family set up and I do not wish to experience that again.
13. Have you ever ruined or sabotaged an opportunity to get married/engaged, because of (fear of rejection, commitment, or another reason)? No.
14. If your answer is "Yes" above please explain. No.
15. Do you feel pressured to get married and have a family from outside sources (ex., family, church, friends, society, etc.)? No.
16. Have you ever felt embarrassed about being over 40 and never been married and no kids? No.
17. Have you had a conversation with God about your situation? No.
18. How do you feel about waiting on God to send you the right husband? I ask God if I must marry then let Him choose the right person for me.
19. Do you believe you would have already been married by now? Why? How? No, because I have never even had a thought of it.
20. Are you okay if you never get married and have children? Do you accept this? Are you content? Why? I would be okay if I don't for now.
21. What advice or words of wisdom would you give to other women in general (whether single or not, with kids or not)? To take life slowly—I mean step by step.
22. Have you ever been tempted to get married or have a child because you got tired of waiting and you felt time was running out? Give examples. No.
23. Have you been engaged or thought you were going to get married and realized it was going to be a big mistake? What happened? Never been engaged.
24. Give examples of how you respond to people who question you as to why you're not married? To stop poking their noses into my affairs.

25. Have you ever thought about what it would be like to be married with children? Kids would have been actively involved in everything I do. I would have to work extra hard both for kids and at work. I don't know if I would have stuck a balance, but it wouldn't be an easy task.

26. Have you ever sabotaged a relationship/dating because you were afraid of getting married/commitment? If so, explain. No, I have not sabotaged.

27. Are you afraid of getting married? If so, why or for what reason(s)? If not, why or for what reason? Yes, I am because of the family set up I grew up in.

28. Have you been in a position where you were in a relationship or engaged to please others, even though, you knew in your heart that was not the right person for you? No.

29. Have you considered adopting a child(ren), foster care, or some other means, if you never give birth to any child(ren) of your own? If so, what option did you consider and why? None of the options.

30. Do you need healing or to come to terms with some pain(s) from the past before you can be open to getting married? Maybe.

31. Have you ever tried online dating to find a mate? If so, what was that experience like? Once and I had a great experience. I quit because I saw it addictive until today, I have not tried it again.

32. Looking back, would you do anything differently? If so, please explain. If not, please explain. I would have strived towards being self-reliant at an early age and not let the luxury of a bad family set up have an impact on my adult life as it is now.

33. For those of you that want to get married, what qualities do you want in a spouse? Handsome, caring and a good communicator.

34. Should a woman who is at least 40 years old, (who dates), be dating for the purpose of getting married? No.

35. How are you living your best life? I am attending golf lessons and also volunteering in an organization.

36. Name some accomplishments, goals, or visions you aspire to complete, have completed, or are working on. Travel more.

37. Is there anything else you would like to say on this subject (being a woman who is at least 40 years old, have never been married before, with no children)? None.

1. Name: Addison P.
2. Country: USA
3. City and/or State: Montana
4. Are you happy/satisfied with being single? No.
5. Are you happy/satisfied with not having any children? Not happy/satisfied.
6. Do you or have you ever envied other women who are married and have a child(ren)? No.
7. When you let others know that you have never been married and have no children, what was their response? What was your response to their response? They don't believe because they say I always look like a man is taking good care of me.
8. What have you learned about being single, with no kids? Never to be stressed with things out of reach.
9. What advice do you have for other women 40 and over, who have never been married and never had children? Appreciate what they have at the moment before they get what they want.
10. For those of you that don't ever want to get married or have children, have you encountered any negativity or criticism about this decision? No.
11. Do you have any regrets? No.
12. Do you choose to be single, with no kids, or is it circumstantial? Please explain. It is circumstantial. I got in an accident at an early age, and it affected my reproductive system.
13. Have you ever ruined or sabotaged an opportunity to get married/engaged, because of (fear of rejection, commitment, or another reason)? No.
14. If your answer is "Yes" above please explain. N/A

15. Do you feel pressured to get married and have a family from outside sources (ex., family, church, friends, society, etc.)? No.

16. Have you ever felt embarrassed about being over 40 and never been married and no kids? No.

17. Have you had a conversation with God about your situation? Yes.

18. How do you feel about waiting on God to send you the right husband? I ask God to provide me with emotional support since was declared that I cannot have kids.

19. Do you believe you would have already been married by now? Why? How? Yes, had it not been for the life-threatening accident I had.

20. Are you okay if you never get married and have children? Do you accept this? Are you content? Why? Not okay but there is nothing much I can do even if I would love to have kids myself.

21. What advice or words of wisdom would you give to other women in general (whether single or not, with kids or not)? Don't do something because society tells you to. If you want to get married, do so because YOU want to, not because your friends/family/peers think you should. The same philosophy should apply to having children. Don't have them because you feel you have to. Do it because you want to. Stop looking to Disney or the latest Romcom to teach you about love and life. There are no set rules. If you're interested in someone, let them know. It's your life to live. Don't live them by anyone else's standards.

22. Have you ever been tempted to get married or have a child because you got tired of waiting and you felt time was running out? Give examples. Never.

23. Have you been engaged or thought you were going to get married and realized it was going to be a big mistake? What happened? I was engaged to someone who was not aware yet of my accident and the possibility of not giving birth. At first, I tried to keep it to myself, but I realized it would be a great mistake and he would realize later into our marriage.

24. Give examples of how you respond to people who question you as to why you're not married? I don't need a partner to prove that I'm worth something.

25. Have you ever thought about what it would be like to be married with children? Getting older and watching your elders start dying off. Then realizing you brought children into this world (you hope they go in there and sleep peacefully), that will go through the pain and suffering that age brings and eventually die. And no matter how wonderful your relationship is, it will end. For myself, I've never been selfish, but one thing I would be selfish about, is hoping I go before my partner, I don't think I could bear seeing them go first.

26. Have you ever sabotaged a relationship/dating because you were afraid of getting married/commitment? If so, explain. Yes, I was once in a relationship where I could not see anything good in my partner and I felt like sabotaging it.

27. Are you afraid of getting married? If so, why or for what reason(s)? If not, why or for what reason? I am afraid of my condition, not marriage.

28. Have you been in a position where you were in a relationship or engaged to please others, even though, you knew in your heart that was not the right person for you? Yes.

29. Have you considered adopting a child(ren), foster care, or some other means, if you never give birth to any child(ren) of your own? If so, what option did you consider and why? Child adoption.

30. Do you need healing or to come to terms with some pain(s) from the past before you can be open to getting married? No.

31. Have you ever tried online dating to find a mate? If so, what was that experience like? Yes, once not good not bad I am neutral on this since everyone has his or her own preferences.

32. Looking back, would you do anything differently? If so, please explain. If not, please explain. Nothing, the past is gone.

33. For those of you that want to get married, what qualities do you want in a spouse? Loving husband.

34. Should a woman who is at least 40 years old, (who dates), be dating for the purpose of getting married? No.

35. How are you living your best life? Going for adventures.

36. Name some accomplishments, goals, or visions you aspire to complete, have completed, or are working on. Attaining my master's degree.

37. Is there anything else you would like to say on this subject (being a woman who is at least 40 years old, have never been married before, with no children)? N/A

1. Name: Brooklyn H.
2. Country: USA
3. City and/or State: Florida
4. Are you happy/satisfied with being single? Yes.
5. Are you happy/satisfied with not having any children? Not happy/satisfied.
6. Do you or have you ever envied other women who are married and have a child(ren)? Yes.
7. When you let others know that you have never been married and have no children, what was their response? What was your response to their response? How come I do not have kids yet? I am still trying.
8. What have you learned about being single, with no kids? Have learned about myself.
9. What advice do you have for other women 40 and over, who have never been married and never had children? They should never lose hope.
10. For those of you that don't ever want to get married or have children, have you encountered any negativity or criticism about this decision? No.
11. Do you have any regrets? No.
12. Do you choose to be single, with no kids, or is it circumstantial? Please explain. All of this is circumstantial.
13. Have you ever ruined or sabotaged an opportunity to get married/engaged, because of (fear of rejection, commitment, or another reason)? No.
14. If your answer is "Yes" above please explain. I have never.
15. Do you feel pressured to get married and have a family from outside sources (ex., family, church, friends, society, etc.)? No.
16. Have you ever felt embarrassed about being over 40 and never been married and no kids? No.

17. Have you had a conversation with God about your situation? Yes.
18. How do you feel about waiting on God to send you the right husband? It feels inspiring.
19. Do you believe you would have already been married by now? Why? How? I do not have any regrets about it.
20. Are you okay if you never get married and have children? Do you accept this? Are you content? Why? I have already come to terms with it.
21. What advice or words of wisdom would you give to other women in general (whether single or not, with kids or not)? Not to lose hope.
22. Have you ever been tempted to get married or have a child because you got tired of waiting and you felt time was running out? Give examples. Never, I am just waiting.
23. Have you been engaged or thought you were going to get married and realized it was going to be a big mistake? What happened? Yes, I have been engaged all along.
24. Give examples of how you respond to people who question you as to why you're not married? That God's time is the best.
25. Have you ever thought about what it would be like to be married with children? Of course, yes, would be enjoyable.
26. Have you ever sabotaged a relationship/dating because you were afraid of getting married/commitment? If so, explain. I tried once but the experience was not good.
27. Are you afraid of getting married? If so, why or for what reason(s)? If not, why or for what reason? I am not afraid.
28. Have you been in a position where you were in a relationship or engaged to please others, even though, you knew in your heart that was not the right person for you? No.
29. Have you considered adopting a child(ren), foster care, or some other means, if you never give birth to any child(ren) of your own? If so, what option did you consider and why? Yes, several times.
30. Do you need healing or to come to terms with some pain(s) from the past before you can be open to getting married? Yes.

31. Have you ever tried online dating to find a mate? If so, what was that experience like? Was never the best experience.
32. Looking back, would you do anything differently? If so, please explain. If not, please explain. I wish I never attempted.
33. For those of you that want to get married, what qualities do you want in a spouse? Honesty, love, and tolerance.
34. Should a woman who is at least 40 years old, (who dates), be dating for the purpose of getting married? Yes.
35. How are you living your best life? Traveling the world.
36. Name some accomplishments, goals, or visions you aspire to complete, have completed, or are working on. Attaining the highest level of education.
37. Is there anything else you would like to say on this subject (being a woman who is at least 40 years old, have never been married before, with no children)? It is not the best experience.

1. Name: Ruby Q.
2. Country: USA
3. City and/or State: Colorado
4. Are you happy/satisfied with being single? Yes.
5. Are you happy/satisfied with not having any children? Yes, I am happy/satisfied.
6. Do you or have you ever envied other women who are married and have a child(ren)? Never.
7. When you let others know that you have never been married and have no children, what was their response? What was your response to their response? They normally encourage me not to despair and I appreciate in response.
8. What have you learned about being single, with no kids? I have learned that kids are heaven sent.

9. What advice do you have for other women 40 and over, who have never been married and never had children? To concentrate on their life and work smart.

10. For those of you that don't ever want to get married or have children, have you encountered any negativity or criticism about this decision? No.

11. Do you have any regrets? No.

12. Do you choose to be single, with no kids, or is it circumstantial? Please explain. I choose to be single with no kids.

13. Have you ever ruined or sabotaged an opportunity to get married/engaged, because of (fear of rejection, commitment, or another reason)? No.

14. If your answer is "Yes" above please explain. N/A

15. Do you feel pressured to get married and have a family from outside sources (ex., family, church, friends, society, etc.)? No.

16. Have you ever felt embarrassed about being over 40 and never been married and no kids? Maybe.

17. Have you had a conversation with God about your situation? Maybe.

18. How do you feel about waiting on God to send you the right husband? God has a masterplan for everyone.

19. Do you believe you would have already been married by now? Why? How? Not really.

20. Are you okay if you never get married and have children? Do you accept this? Are you content? Why? Yes, I would be content provided it was God's plan.

21. What advice or words of wisdom would you give to other women in general (whether single or not, with kids or not)? To have tolerance and respect with one another regardless of marital status.

22. Have you ever been tempted to get married or have a child because you got tired of waiting and you felt time was running out? Give examples. Yes.

23. Have you been engaged or thought you were going to get married and realized it was going to be a big mistake? What happened? No.

24. Give examples of how you respond to people who question you as to why you're not married? I say, "Why should we not talk about job promotion instead".

25. Have you ever thought about what it would be like to be married with children? It would have been hectic.

26. Have you ever sabotaged a relationship/dating because you were afraid of getting married/commitment? If so, explain. Yes, I sabotaged once. The guy was a little bit of a joker.

27. Are you afraid of getting married? If so, why or for what reason(s)? If not, why or for what reason? Yes, I am afraid getting married to jokers.

28. Have you been in a position where you were in a relationship or engaged to please others, even though, you knew in your heart that was not the right person for you? No.

29. Have you considered adopting a child(ren), foster care, or some other means, if you never give birth to any child(ren) of your own? If so, what option did you consider and why? Foster Care.

30. Do you need healing or to come to terms with some pain(s) from the past before you can be open to getting married? No.

31. Have you ever tried online dating to find a mate? If so, what was that experience like? Never.

32. Looking back, would you do anything differently? If so, please explain. If not, please explain. I don't bother much about my past.

33. For those of you that want to get married, what qualities do you want in a spouse? A humble husband would be ideal.

34. Should a woman who is at least 40 years old, (who dates), be dating for the purpose of getting married? No.

35. How are you living your best life? I love basketball.

36. Name some accomplishments, goals, or visions you aspire to complete, have completed, or are working on. Enrollment into law school.

37. Is there anything else you would like to say on this subject (being a woman who is at least 40 years old, have never been married before, with no children)? God is the giver of kids.

1. Name: Autumn K.
2. Country: USA
3. City and/or State: Georgia
4. Are you happy/satisfied with being single? Yes.
5. Are you happy/satisfied with not having any children? Yes, I am happy/satisfied.
6. Do you or have you ever envied other women who are married and have a child(ren)? Never.
7. When you let others know that you have never been married and have no children, what was their response? What was your response to their response? (No answer).
8. What have you learned about being single, with no kids? You can still have your own cake and eat it.
9. What advice do you have for other women 40 and over, who have never been married and never had children? Life is a gift-a one-time opportunity. Our aim should be to appreciate every single bit of it. The basic human tendency is to stay depressed and helpless. It takes some effort in raising your morale and sustaining it. That my friend, is what life is all about. You will be crucified many times, but you have to resurrect yourself like a phoenix bird. Life is awesome, don't let anyone or anything take the positivity out of it. Have a hobby. Travel alone. Fall in love. Take yourself away from those social networking sites full of narcissists and busy cities. Do gardening, wake up early in the morning and watch the sunrise. Read books. Go for long drives. Try and taste different cuisines. Do whatever makes you happy (except for certain indulgences with serious health hazards). Never sit idle or sleep lazily. Always keep occupied. For me, I love nature and am constantly awed and amazed by what it can do. That inspired me to take interest in photography, painting, music and composing, writing, etc. There are always things that would make you happy right around you. It's just that you have to make some effort to

appreciate it, even if it's a simple gesture like buying food for a homeless guy or picking up a fallen toy for a kid.

10. For those of you that don't ever want to get married or have children, have you encountered any negativity or criticism about this decision? No.

11. Do you have any regrets? No.

12. Do you choose to be single, with no kids, or is it circumstantial? Please explain. I choose too. For a start, we should recognize that the idea of being deeply in love with one special partner over a whole lifetime, what we can call romantic love, is a very new, ambitious, and odd concept, which is at best 250 years old.

13. Have you ever ruined or sabotaged an opportunity to get married/engaged, because of (fear of rejection, commitment, or another reason)? No.

14. If your answer is "Yes" above please explain. N/A

15. Do you feel pressured to get married and have a family from outside sources (ex., family, church, friends, society, etc.)? No.

16. Have you ever felt embarrassed about being over 40 and never been married and no kids? Maybe.

17. Have you had a conversation with God about your situation? Maybe.

18. How do you feel about waiting on God to send you the right husband? God is omnipotent.

19. Do you believe you would have already been married by now? Why? How? Yes, I do.

20. Are you okay if you never get married and have children? Do you accept this? Are you content? Why? If that is destiny, then so be it.

21. What advice or words of wisdom would you give to other women in general (whether single or not, with kids or not)? You live your life only once. So, it is very necessary to spend it usefully. Don't think going for movies and having fun is enjoying life. It is what everyone does. You should have an aim in your life. You should work towards it. When you are focused, you will definitely achieve your aim. The happiness you feel when you achieve your goal is the true enjoyment in your life. Spending quality time

with your spouse and children gives you real enjoyment. Helping the needy gives you a satisfying enjoyment. Do you know being honest, makes you feel you are a good person? This feeling that you are a good person gives you fulfillment, and fulfillment in life is also true enjoyment.

22. Have you ever been tempted to get married or have a child because you got tired of waiting and you felt time was running out? Give examples. Yes, my ex once wanted us to have a bond and he felt time was not on our side. I declined since I wasn't ready.

23. Have you been engaged or thought you were going to get married and realized it was going to be a big mistake? What happened? Yes, in my twenties, with my ex-boyfriend, who started asking for sex and I felt awkward in the relationship.

24. Give examples of how you respond to people who question you as to why you're not married? I tell them those are my personal information that I am not comfortable sharing with them.

25. Have you ever thought about what it would be like to be married with children? Fun.

26. Have you ever sabotaged a relationship/dating because you were afraid of getting married/commitment? If so, explain. Yes, as explained previously.

27. Are you afraid of getting married? If so, why or for what reason(s)? If not, why or for what reason? Not afraid.

28. Have you been in a position where you were in a relationship or engaged to please others, even though, you knew in your heart that was not the right person for you? Yes.

29. Have you considered adopting a child(ren), foster care, or some other means, if you never give birth to any child(ren) of your own? If so, what option did you consider and why? Adoption.

30. Do you need healing or to come to terms with some pain(s) from the past before you can be open to getting married? No.

31. Have you ever tried online dating to find a mate? If so, what was that experience like? Yes.

32. Looking back, would you do anything differently? If so, please explain. If not, please explain. Nothing.

33. For those of you that want to get married, what qualities do you want in a spouse? Kindness, patience, understanding, empathy, and compassion.

34. Should a woman who is at least 40 years old, (who dates), be dating for the purpose of getting married? No.

35. How are you living your best life? Helping the needy and homeless.

36. Name some accomplishments, goals, or visions you aspire to complete, have completed, or are working on. I aspire to graduate by spring with a doctorate degree.

37. Is there anything else you would like to say on this subject (being a woman who is at least 40 years old, have never been married before, with no children)? Just some advice to this group: You will enjoy life when you are not completely dependent on anyone!

1. Name: Hailey B.
2. Country: USA
3. City and/or State: Texas
4. Are you happy/satisfied with being single? No.
5. Are you happy/satisfied with not having any children? Not happy/satisfied.
6. Do you or have you ever envied other women who are married and have a child(ren)? No.
7. When you let others know that you have never been married and have no children, what was their response? What was your response to their response? I tell them it's my life.
8. What have you learned about being single, with no kids? Kids are a blessing.
9. What advice do you have for other women 40 and over, who have never been married and never had children? Not to envy.
10. For those of you that don't ever want to get married or have children, have you encountered any negativity or criticism about this decision? No.
11. Do you have any regrets? No.
12. Do you choose to be single, with no kids, or is it circumstantial? Please explain. My choice.
13. Have you ever ruined or sabotaged an opportunity to get married/engaged, because of (fear of rejection, commitment, or another reason)? No.
14. If your answer is "Yes" above please explain. No.
15. Do you feel pressured to get married and have a family from outside sources (ex., family, church, friends, society, etc.)? No.
16. Have you ever felt embarrassed about being over 40 and never been married and no kids? Yes.
17. Have you had a conversation with God about your situation? No.

18. How do you feel about waiting on God to send you the right husband? God is the creator of the universe and may his will prevail.

19. Do you believe you would have already been married by now? Why? How? No.

20. Are you okay if you never get married and have children? Do you accept this? Are you content? Why? I will accept.

21. What advice or words of wisdom would you give to other women in general (whether single or not, with kids or not)? Women should be good ambassadors and protect fellow women.

22. Have you ever been tempted to get married or have a child because you got tired of waiting and you felt time was running out? Give examples. Never.

23. Have you been engaged or thought you were going to get married and realized it was going to be a big mistake? What happened? No engagement yet.

24. Give examples of how you respond to people who question you as to why you're not married? (No answer).

25. Have you ever thought about what it would be like to be married with children? No.

26. Have you ever sabotaged a relationship/dating because you were afraid of getting married/commitment? If so, explain. No.

27. Are you afraid of getting married? If so, why or for what reason(s)? If not, why or for what reason? Yes, I am afraid because of what I hear from married people.

28. Have you been in a position where you were in a relationship or engaged to please others, even though, you knew in your heart that was not the right person for you? No.

29. Have you considered adopting a child(ren), foster care, or some other means, if you never give birth to any child(ren) of your own? If so, what option did you consider and why? Foster care.

30. Do you need healing or to come to terms with some pain(s) from the past before you can be open to getting married? No.

31. Have you ever tried online dating to find a mate? If so, what was that experience like? Yes, when Tinder was still new. I was

asked to pay to access some features and I was like, why should I pay to access some random strangers.

32. Looking back, would you do anything differently? If so, please explain. If not, please explain. Perhaps, I would have attended social functions often.

33. For those of you that want to get married, what qualities do you want in a spouse? Kind and faithful.

34. Should a woman who is at least 40 years old, (who dates), be dating for the purpose of getting married? Yes.

35. How are you living your best life? Adventure and helping the needy in society.

36. Name some accomplishments, goals, or visions you aspire to complete, have completed, or are working on. I have my own children's home.

37. Is there anything else you would like to say on this subject (being a woman who is at least 40 years old, have never been married before, with no children)? No.

1. Name: Emery C.
2. Country: USA
3. City and/or State: Chicago
4. Are you happy/satisfied with being single? Yes.
5. Are you happy/satisfied with not having any children? Yes, I am happy/satisfied.
6. Do you or have you ever envied other women who are married and have a child(ren)? Never.
7. When you let others know that you have never been married and have no children, what was their response? What was your response to their response? (No answer).
8. What have you learned about being single, with no kids? It is not good for man to live alone.

9. What advice do you have for other women 40 and over, who have never been married and never had children? To be strong.
10. For those of you that don't ever want to get married or have children, have you encountered any negativity or criticism about this decision? Yes.
11. Do you have any regrets? No.
12. Do you choose to be single, with no kids, or is it circumstantial? Please explain. I choose single life.
13. Have you ever ruined or sabotaged an opportunity to get married/engaged, because of (fear of rejection, commitment, or another reason)? No.
14. If your answer is "Yes" above please explain. N/A
15. Do you feel pressured to get married and have a family from outside sources (ex., family, church, friends, society, etc.)? No.
16. Have you ever felt embarrassed about being over 40 and never been married and no kids? No.
17. Have you had a conversation with God about your situation? Maybe.
18. How do you feel about waiting on God to send you the right husband? God gives people what they seek.
19. Do you believe you would have already been married by now? Why? How? No.
20. Are you okay if you never get married and have children? Do you accept this? Are you content? Why? Yes, I will still be okay.
21. What advice or words of wisdom would you give to other women in general (whether single or not, with kids or not)? To work hard and be better versions of themselves.
22. Have you ever been tempted to get married or have a child because you got tired of waiting and you felt time was running out? Give examples. Yes, by my friend, but I managed to maneuver.
23. Have you been engaged or thought you were going to get married and realized it was going to be a big mistake? What happened? Yes, and I ended the relationship on mutual basis.
24. Give examples of how you respond to people who question you as to why you're not married? I tell them it is on my list of things to do the following year.

25. Have you ever thought about what it would be like to be married with children? Yes, and I know children are playful it would still be fun and tedious at the same time.
26. Have you ever sabotaged a relationship/dating because you were afraid of getting married/commitment? If so, explain. No.
27. Are you afraid of getting married? If so, why or for what reason(s)? If not, why or for what reason? Yes, I am afraid. Too used to my freedom.
28. Have you been in a position where you were in a relationship or engaged to please others, even though, you knew in your heart that was not the right person for you? No.
29. Have you considered adopting a child(ren), foster care, or some other means, if you never give birth to any child(ren) of your own? If so, what option did you consider and why? Adopting maybe.
30. Do you need healing or to come to terms with some pain(s) from the past before you can be open to getting married? No.
31. Have you ever tried online dating to find a mate? If so, what was that experience like? Once.
32. Looking back, would you do anything differently? If so, please explain. If not, please explain. I would have perhaps become a pastor.
33. For those of you that want to get married, what qualities do you want in a spouse? Do not want to.
34. Should a woman who is at least 40 years old, (who dates), be dating for the purpose of getting married? No.
35. How are you living your best life? Playing hockey with my friends and exercising.
36. Name some accomplishments, goals, or visions you aspire to complete, have completed, or are working on. Finished a marathon for charity.
37. Is there anything else you would like to say on this subject (being a woman who is at least 40 years old, have never been married before, with no children)? N/A

1. Name: Brielle E.
2. Country: USA
3. City and/or State: Georgia
4. Are you happy/satisfied with being single? No.
5. Are you happy/satisfied with not having any children? Not happy/satisfied.
6. Do you or have you ever envied other women who are married and have a child(ren)? No.
7. When you let others know that you have never been married and have no children, what was their response? What was your response to their response? They tell me pointblank to get myself a husband.
8. What have you learned about being single, with no kids? I have learned the value of having a friend who comes through for me.
9. What advice do you have for other women 40 and over, who have never been married and never had children? To do whatever makes them happy.
10. For those of you that don't ever want to get married or have children, have you encountered any negativity or criticism about this decision? No.
11. Do you have any regrets? No.
12. Do you choose to be single, with no kids, or is it circumstantial? Please explain. It is circumstantial.
13. Have you ever ruined or sabotaged an opportunity to get married/engaged, because of (fear of rejection, commitment, or another reason)? No.
14. If your answer is "Yes" above please explain. N/A
15. Do you feel pressured to get married and have a family from outside sources (ex., family, church, friends, society, etc.)? No.
16. Have you ever felt embarrassed about being over 40 and never been married and no kids? No.

17. Have you had a conversation with God about your situation? No.
18. How do you feel about waiting on God to send you the right husband? God is a listening.
19. Do you believe you would have already been married by now? Why? How? Not really.
20. Are you okay if you never get married and have children? Do you accept this? Are you content? Why? I will be content.
21. What advice or words of wisdom would you give to other women in general (whether single or not, with kids or not)? Love one another and strive towards excellence.
22. Have you ever been tempted to get married or have a child because you got tired of waiting and you felt time was running out? Give examples. No.
23. Have you been engaged or thought you were going to get married and realized it was going to be a big mistake? What happened? No.
24. Give examples of how you respond to people who question you as to why you're not married? I ask them to change the topic.
25. Have you ever thought about what it would be like to be married with children? No, I haven't been a fan of marriage.
26. Have you ever sabotaged a relationship/dating because you were afraid of getting married/commitment? If so, explain. Not really.
27. Are you afraid of getting married? If so, why or for what reason(s)? If not, why or for what reason? Yes, I am afraid of commitment.
28. Have you been in a position where you were in a relationship or engaged to please others, even though, you knew in your heart that was not the right person for you? No.
29. Have you considered adopting a child(ren), foster care, or some other means, if you never give birth to any child(ren) of your own? If so, what option did you consider and why? Foster.
30. Do you need healing or to come to terms with some pain(s) from the past before you can be open to getting married? No.

31. Have you ever tried online dating to find a mate? If so, what was that experience like? Never.

32. Looking back, would you do anything differently? If so, please explain. If not, please explain. If you want to be successful forget about past events.

33. For those of you that want to get married, what qualities do you want in a spouse? Honesty and Humility.

34. Should a woman who is at least 40 years old, (who dates), be dating for the purpose of getting married? No.

35. How are you living your best life? Touring the world and road trips.

36. Name some accomplishments, goals, or visions you aspire to complete, have completed, or are working on. Visit Masaai Mara or Serengeti for wildebeest migration.

37. Is there anything else you would like to say on this subject (being a woman who is at least 40 years old, have never been married before, with no children)? No.

1. Name: Suzanna I.
2. Country: United States
3. City and/or State: Pantego, North Carolina
4. Are you happy/satisfied with being single? Maybe.
5. Are you happy/satisfied with not having any children? Yes, I am happy/satisfied.
6. Do you or have you ever envied other women who are married and have a child(ren)? I would have liked to have children, but I am happy where the Lord has placed me. I don't envy married women. Couldn't very well envy a woman if I didn't want their man and surely don't. I would rather have had children and thought about adopting, but that didn't work out. At this point, I would like to have grandchildren more than children!
7. When you let others know that you have never been married and have no children, what was their response? What was your response to their response? Some people say, "You're the smart one!" May say, "I wouldn't say that." Some say, "How did you escape?" To that I said, "It wasn't easy!"
8. What have you learned about being single, with no kids? You need to reach out to other people when you don't have your own family.
9. What advice do you have for other women 40 and over, who have never been married and never had children? Be yourself. Embrace your freedom! Find your joy in the Lord since you won't have it from husband and children. You can be happy and satisfied wherever the Lord has placed you.
10. For those of you that don't ever want to get married or have children, have you encountered any negativity or criticism about this decision? (No answer).
11. Do you have any regrets? No.
12. Do you choose to be single, with no kids, or is it circumstantial? Please explain. I assumed I would get married when the time was

right and the right man came along, but it just never happened. Have never met an eligible man who really seemed to fit with me very well. "The most important components of love are friendship, devotion and intellectual compatibility" or in other words, body, soul, and spirit. I have found two out of the three, but never, but never all three in one man. For instance, I have met a man who was a great friend, was attractive physically, but he wasn't a Christian. Or, I have seen guys who were good Christians and nice enough but no physical attraction.

13. Have you ever ruined or sabotaged an opportunity to get married/engaged, because of (fear of rejection, commitment, or another reason)? No.

14. If your answer is "Yes" above please explain. There have been plenty of "opportunities", but as I mentioned they didn't seem right.

15. Do you feel pressured to get married and have a family from outside sources (ex., family, church, friends, society, etc.)? No.

16. Have you ever felt embarrassed about being over 40 and never been married and no kids? No.

17. Have you had a conversation with God about your situation? Yes.

18. How do you feel about waiting on God to send you the right husband? That is the only appropriate course of action. The man is to be the spiritual leader and that includes romance. Though not sure what I would do if I actually ever met someone who seemed perfect, and he didn't get the idea. But that has never happened.

19. Do you believe you would have already been married by now? Why? How? Not sure I understand this question. There were lots of men who seemed to think I was the one for them, but I didn't.

20. Are you okay if you never get married and have children? Do you accept this? Are you content? Why? Yes. I want whatever God's plan is for my life. I've done okay so far so probably will continue to be able to survive with only God, though it is harder now that my parents are gone.

21. What advice or words of wisdom would you give to other women in general (whether single or not, with kids or not)?

"Submit thy way unto the Lord. Trust also in Him and He shall bring it to pass."

22. Have you ever been tempted to get married or have a child because you got tired of waiting and you felt time was running out? Give examples. My friend's husband, with her consent approached me about having his child by AI because she was too old, and he wanted a child. He had a nice plan for support etc., but I wasn't that tempted because I didn't want too much to do with him. Had I known that he would die in a few years I might have been more tempted.

23. Have you been engaged or thought you were going to get married and realized it was going to be a big mistake? What happened? I had two men I was dating at different times who were talking marriage but the one didn't want to stay in the church and the other was too controlling. He thought he could tell me how to act in personal areas of my life, and even tell me what to think.

24. Give examples of how you respond to people who question you as to why you're not married? As I mentioned, body soul and spirit need to be compatible, and I've never found one who had all three. My friend tells people that this is God's will for her life, and that God has given her the gift of singleness.

25. Have you ever thought about what it would be like to be married with children? Of course!

26. Have you ever sabotaged a relationship/dating because you were afraid of getting married/commitment? If so, explain. No.

27. Are you afraid of getting married? If so, why or for what reason(s)? If not, why or for what reason? No.

28. Have you been in a position where you were in a relationship or engaged to please others, even though, you knew in your heart that was not the right person for you? No.

29. Have you considered adopting a child(ren), foster care, or some other means, if you never give birth to any child(ren) of your own? If so, what option did you consider and why? I considered both, but I wasn't approved for foster care if I didn't have higher outside income, and thought it made no sense to have a child

and put it to a babysitter five days a week to go out and work. I had custody of two babies and considered adoption, but the time didn't seem to be right. I said if I was ever given a third, I would keep it, but was never given the third.

30. Do you need healing or to come to terms with some pain(s) from the past before you can be open to getting married? No.

31. Have you ever tried online dating to find a mate? If so, what was that experience like? No.

32. Looking back, would you do anything differently? If so, please explain. If not, please explain. Probably not.

33. For those of you that want to get married, what qualities do you want in a spouse? Honest, kind, stable.

34. Should a woman who is at least 40 years old, (who dates), be dating for the purpose of getting married? Yes. It depends on your definition of dating. If you are having a "romance," the ultimate goal would be marriage. But I have male friends I interact with, maybe even go out to eat, but we aren't dating. We are just friends and there is no romance in it.

35. How are you living your best life? I enjoy travel, photography, books, the beauties of nature, many things. In fact, I expect that I enjoy my life more than most people, single or married!

36. Name some accomplishments, goals, or visions you aspire to complete, have completed, or are working on. I have a book about ready to publish. I bought a building and intend to start a lending library for the community.

37. Is there anything else you would like to say on this subject (being a woman who is at least 40 years old, have never been married before, with no children)? I think that people looking down their nose at you, or leaving you out, are some of the worst things about being single. But it's not bad enough to get married just to avoid it. In the sight of the Lord, we are all valuable, and those who don't understand that are only hurting themselves.

1. Name: Lydia T.
2. Country:
3. City and/or State: Virginia
4. Are you happy/satisfied with being single? Yes.
5. Are you happy/satisfied with not having any children? Yes, I am happy/satisfied.
6. Do you or have you ever envied other women who are married and have a child(ren)? No.
7. When you let others know that you have never been married and have no children, what was their response? What was your response to their response? Wonder how come with all the qualities I have.
8. What have you learned about being single, with no kids? I learned as much about myself less what I could have learned about myself when I was in a relationship.
9. What advice do you have for other women 40 and over, who have never been married and never had children? This is a man's world. It is unfair. Ungrateful. Unequal. You will have to fight for what is right. And by fight, I mean use your heart, head and human spirit is getting things done. Not force, noise or violence.
10. For those of you that don't ever want to get married or have children, have you encountered any negativity or criticism about this decision? No.
11. Do you have any regrets? No.
12. Do you choose to be single, with no kids, or is it circumstantial? Please explain. Choice.
13. Have you ever ruined or sabotaged an opportunity to get married/engaged, because of (fear of rejection, commitment, or another reason)? No.
14. If your answer is "Yes" above please explain. N/A
15. Do you feel pressured to get married and have a family from outside sources (ex., family, church, friends, society, etc.)? No.

16. Have you ever felt embarrassed about being over 40 and never been married and no kids? No.

17. Have you had a conversation with God about your situation? Maybe.

18. How do you feel about waiting on God to send you the right husband? God is there for everyone, and He works with a plan.

19. Do you believe you would have already been married by now? Why? How? Yes.

20. Are you okay if you never get married and have children? Do you accept this? Are you content? Why? Okay.

21. What advice or words of wisdom would you give to other women in general (whether single or not, with kids or not)? Never trust any man. Most men look at women as sex objects. If any man is nice to you-be cautious.

22. Have you ever been tempted to get married or have a child because you got tired of waiting and you felt time was running out? Give examples. No.

23. Have you been engaged or thought you were going to get married and realized it was going to be a big mistake? What happened? Never.

24. Give examples of how you respond to people who question you as to why you're not married? (No answer).

25. Have you ever thought about what it would be like to be married with children? No.

26. Have you ever sabotaged a relationship/dating because you were afraid of getting married/commitment? If so, explain. Never.

27. Are you afraid of getting married? If so, why or for what reason(s)? If not, why or for what reason? Not afraid.

28. Have you been in a position where you were in a relationship or engaged to please others, even though, you knew in your heart that was not the right person for you? Maybe.

29. Have you considered adopting a child(ren), foster care, or some other means, if you never give birth to any child(ren) of your own? If so, what option did you consider and why? Adoption, yes.

30. Do you need healing or to come to terms with some pain(s) from the past before you can be open to getting married? No.

31. Have you ever tried online dating to find a mate? If so, what was that experience like? I've been trying online dating for a few months now—mostly Tinder but also OK Cupid and Bumble. It's been an interesting experience.
32. Looking back, would you do anything differently? If so, please explain. If not, please explain. None.
33. For those of you that want to get married, what qualities do you want in a spouse? Not at all.
34. Should a woman who is at least 40 years old, (who dates), be dating for the purpose of getting married? No.
35. How are you living your best life? Exploring different parts of the world.
36. Name some accomplishments, goals, or visions you aspire to complete, have completed, or are working on. I have travelled over 50 countries.
37. Is there anything else you would like to say on this subject (being a woman who is at least 40 years old, have never been married before, with no children)? No answer.

1. Name: Tibbie M.
2. Country: USA
3. City and/or State: New York
4. Are you happy/satisfied with being single? No.
5. Are you happy/satisfied with not having any children? Not happy/satisfied.
6. Do you or have you ever envied other women who are married and have a child(ren)? Not before.
7. When you let others know that you have never been married and have no children, what was their response? What was your response to their response? I try as much as possible to hide my marital status from people and in the event, it is revealed, I say I have not been lucky to meet Mr. Right.

8. What have you learned about being single, with no kids? The best thing I learned is that I must and do appreciate my life and the time that I have for myself. I cannot imagine the lives of mothers, including mine, who spend their life worrying about their children. Maybe, I do not have such strength. The wives or girlfriends who worry or get hurt because of their husbands/boyfriends/their choices/circumstances and vice versa. I may not possess any strength to face such problems as well. Or you know not being able to do anything that you want to do like travelling, napping, watching movies, etc., because your husband or boyfriend says no. I am not always happy being single. I have to face a lot of things alone. One of the worse things are like being mocked for being single, having to tolerate or having to deal with married superiors who bully me, but yes, I must and do appreciate my life.

9. What advice do you have for other women 40 and over, who have never been married and never had children? (No Answer).

10. For those of you that don't ever want to get married or have children, have you encountered any negativity or criticism about this decision? Yes.

11. Do you have any regrets? Maybe.

12. Do you choose to be single, with no kids, or is it circumstantial? Please explain. I guess you could say both. I've had relationships that did not work out for one reason or another. I decided to stay alone for a while to clear my head and just have some alone time. It started off with one year and became more. Except for a few casual dates, that's how single I've been. I'm a loner by nature, so it hasn't been hard. In fact, I like it and I find that even my best relationships have been exhausting. I'm open to meeting someone, but he better be darn perfect, or I won't invest my time.

13. Have you ever ruined or sabotaged an opportunity to get married/engaged, because of (fear of rejection, commitment, or another reason)? No.

14. If your answer is "Yes" above please explain. N/A

15. Do you feel pressured to get married and have a family from outside sources (ex., family, church, friends, society, etc.)? No.

16. Have you ever felt embarrassed about being over 40 and never been married and no kids? No.
17. Have you had a conversation with God about your situation? Yes.
18. How do you feel about waiting on God to send you the right husband? God is a wonderful God and has the masterplan for my life.
19. Do you believe you would have already been married by now? Why? How? Yes, because I put my eggs in the wrong basket. Then I barked up the wrong tree then I settled for the apple that fell from the wrong tree. I attract the wrong people…and make the wrong choices…but I didn't think I would be 40 and unmarried and I don't hide the fact that I am bitter about it… basically my attitude is the choice that keeps me unmarried in these circumstances.
20. Are you okay if you never get married and have children? Do you accept this? Are you content? Why? Not at all.
21. What advice or words of wisdom would you give to other women in general (whether single or not, with kids or not)? Dating under the age of 19 is useless and serious.
22. Have you ever been tempted to get married or have a child because you got tired of waiting and you felt time was running out? Give examples. My parents tried to force me to get married when I was 28. I finished my degree, got a job, and moved out of their house.
23. Have you been engaged or thought you were going to get married and realized it was going to be a big mistake? What happened? For all the right reasons, I thought. He was gainfully employed, had the same level of education, wanted kids, was just 4 years older than me, shared my interests in film, culture, music, was well spoken and loved me. Turned out he lied about his education, lied about wanting kids, lied about screenwriting, had never made a film, or understood filmmaking, the only opera he knew was the one he had taken me to see, was stuck at his job, was possessive and very jealous, wanted me to take care of his parents. I was deceived and was not one of those women who was

going to get pregnant when the father didn't want a kid. I was born to two people who wanted me, and I know what a happy marriage and healthy partnership looked like. I didn't have one. My heart was broken, but I recovered.

24. Give examples of how you respond to people who question you as to why you're not married? I know I always put everyone ahead of me and this is the reason: I will sacrifice all my dreams and happiness for others and will behave as a robot. I don't want that. I want to live myself and want to love myself. I have gone through a lot in my entire life and now I can't bear anymore. I just want peace in my life. I don't want anyone to expect anything from me. I don't want any burden. Maybe I am sounding a bit selfish but trust me only I know what I have faced, so please don't judge me. Mom and dad, I love you and will not do anything wrong. I don't want to marry because I don't want to eliminate the real me.

25. Have you ever thought about what it would be like to be married with children? Of course, lively environment full of love in the air. Can't stop imagining.

26. Have you ever sabotaged a relationship/dating because you were afraid of getting married/commitment? If so, explain. Yes because of malice and lies. I was afraid and had to sabotage.

27. Are you afraid of getting married? If so, why or for what reason(s)? If not, why or for what reason? Yes.

28. Have you been in a position where you were in a relationship or engaged to please others, even though, you knew in your heart that was not the right person for you? Yes.

29. Have you considered adopting a child(ren), foster care, or some other means, if you never give birth to any child(ren) of your own? If so, what option did you consider and why? Foster care for me.

30. Do you need healing or to come to terms with some pain(s) from the past before you can be open to getting married? Yes.

31. Have you ever tried online dating to find a mate? If so, what was that experience like? I have probably used sites like Match, POF and OK Cupid a grand total of six years and maybe went out

with 14 people during that time—a little over two per year. Some people get the luck of the draw and meet their future spouses two or three clicks in. That was not true for me, and yeah, I consider it poor luck and bad decision-making in one case. I met four I found intriguing; three of those four had honorable intentions insofar that they were looking for a committed partnership (marriage). Otherwise, I got men who were still married and living with their wives, men who just got divorced and weren't ready to date, (although they were in denial about it), and men who didn't seem to grasp what made for a healthy relationship or in fact have a clue why they were there. Okay, they had one clue. Got two alcoholics (there was a lot of overlap between drinkers and still married/recently divorced) and one who was such an incredible oddball, it was pretty clear why he'd remain single for the rest of his life. Of the three potential same-age peers, two lived out of state and one I dumbly dinged because he had kids in college. He could have been a keeper, and in fact, is happily remarried today. Instead, I inadvertently chose a player—a "nice" one, but still cagey—and frittered away a respectable amount of time. That was a learning lesson on a very steep bell curve. Unfortunately, it's men and women like these that make desirable single people extremely way of doing the online dating shuffle again and cause us to drop out of it entirely. If I had to go back and do things differently, I would have chosen the single dad and seen if that played out. We knew some of the same people, and he checked out okay. Sometimes huge incompatibilities can be worked around if you meet someone who treats you with caring, kindness, and respect. So, my take-away from online dating is that you're at a disadvantage when the person you go out with isn't a part of your social circle. When you already know someone through our existing network, you have a fairly reliable perception of that person's reputation, belief system, romantic history, etc., and you can make a more informed choice. True story: I encountered one guy on OK Cupid, and I knew someone he knew, so I emailed the acquaintance, who told me DON'T DO IT, IT'S A TRAP! As it turns out, the man had acquired a reputation of extorting women for money and then pulling a disappearing act. So, you have to vet the people you meet through online dating sites quite thoroughly and determine if everything they tell you about themselves checks out. Those who are serious about getting serious won't mind being vetted.

32. Looking back, would you do anything differently? If so, please explain. If not, please explain. As said, if I had to go back and do things differently, I would have chosen the single dad and seen if that played out. We knew some of the same people, and he checked out okay. Sometimes huge incompatibilities can be worked around if you meet someone who treats you with caring, kindness, and respect.

33. For those of you that want to get married, what qualities do you want in a spouse? I want him to be kind and understanding. Mostly mature.

34. Should a woman who is at least 40 years old, (who dates), be dating for the purpose of getting married? Yes.

35. How are you living your best life? Going to church and reading novels.

36. Name some accomplishments, goals, or visions you aspire to complete, have completed, or are working on. Recently enrolled for my MBA.

37. Is there anything else you would like to say on this subject (being a woman who is at least 40 years old, have never been married before, with no children)? No.

1. Name: Renie C.
2. Country: Singapore
3. City and/or State: Boon Lay Place
4. Are you happy/satisfied with being single? Yes.
5. Are you happy/satisfied with not having any children? Yes, I am happy/satisfied.

6. Do you or have you ever envied other women who are married and have a child(ren)? No.

7. When you let others know that you have never been married and have no children, what was their response? What was your response to their response? It feels like a slap in the face, as most usually mock me forgetting that it is my personal decision not to get married.

8. What have you learned about being single, with no kids? Better to feel lonely now and again but have lots of choices and not live your life for someone else or be let down.

9. What advice do you have for other women 40 and over, who have never been married and never had children? Your problem is your problem not anyone else's problem, cause at the end of the day, once you are with yourself, no one cares.

10. For those of you that don't ever want to get married or have children, have you encountered any negativity or criticism about this decision? Yes.

11. Do you have any regrets? Maybe.

12. Do you choose to be single, with no kids, or is it circumstantial? Please explain. I think that it is very difficult for some people to understand why there are some individuals that choose a different path than others, especially if those choices go against the social norm. Over here in Singapore, most of us, at some point or another, may date, marry, have children, have a golden retriever, a nice little house, and a white picket fence. That is what some may picture as their dream, but it doesn't have to be your dream, and if your dream looks different that is nothing to be ashamed of. I personally never wanted to marry, and simply because I think it is very difficult for some individuals to connect on a certain level to make the relationship stable. I was also feeling pressure from my grandparents and church members at various times for not getting married or even going on a date with someone. But I refused to date out of convenience or because it makes other people feel more comfortable. I have turned down several people, and some of them were very successful, good looking, and goodhearted individuals, but the fact of the matter is that I

am simply happier when I am free with my life and retain that autonomy. I am more productive on my own, I push myself more, and I strive to push myself to the farthest extent my potential allows. I am happy with my method, and I know that it works for me because I ask myself these four things: 1.) Am I happy? 2.) Am I healthy? 3.) Am I proud of what I'm doing in life? 4.) And am I proud of the person I'm becoming?

13. Have you ever ruined or sabotaged an opportunity to get married/engaged, because of (fear of rejection, commitment, or another reason)? No.

14. If your answer is "Yes" above please explain. N/A

15. Do you feel pressured to get married and have a family from outside sources (ex., family, church, friends, society, etc.)? No.

16. Have you ever felt embarrassed about being over 40 and never been married and no kids? No.

17. Have you had a conversation with God about your situation? Yes.

18. How do you feel about waiting on God to send you the right husband? The difficulty here is that the concept of praying is inherently biased. If you pray for something and it happens, then that is seen as God answering that prayer. If it doesn't happen then it as seen as the person praying isn't devout enough, or similar.

19. Do you believe you would have already been married by now? Why? How? If I had a change of plans and priorities, then I would be married by now.

20. Are you okay if you never get married and have children? Do you accept this? Are you content? Why? Very comfortable and okay.

21. What advice or words of wisdom would you give to other women in general (whether single or not, with kids or not)? Always use the "KISS" principle. Keep It Short and Sweet! Then head for marriage. Never assume the guy will stick with you forever without any commitment. It is not the nature of men to be so – thanks to nature.

22. Have you ever been tempted to get married or have a child because you got tired of waiting and you felt time was running

out? Give examples. Yes, my grandparents once did without respecting my choices in life. Everyone has different choices and dreams.

23. Have you been engaged or thought you were going to get married and realized it was going to be a big mistake? What happened? Getting married is always a mistake. Not all marriages end in divorce, but all divorces start in marriage. If you have any doubts, any at all, no matter how small, DO NOT GET MARRIED.

24. Give examples of how you respond to people who question you as to why you're not married? It is difficult to admit, but I can't lie to you.

25. Have you ever thought about what it would be like to be married with children? I don't have kids and I'm happy.

26. Have you ever sabotaged a relationship/dating because you were afraid of getting married/commitment? If so, explain. No.

27. Are you afraid of getting married? If so, why or for what reason(s)? If not, why or for what reason? I am scared because I know it will not work out for me.

28. Have you been in a position where you were in a relationship or engaged to please others, even though, you knew in your heart that was not the right person for you? No.

29. Have you considered adopting a child(ren), foster care, or some other means, if you never give birth to any child(ren) of your own? If so, what option did you consider and why? None.

30. Do you need healing or to come to terms with some pain(s) from the past before you can be open to getting married? Maybe.

31. Have you ever tried online dating to find a mate? If so, what was that experience like? Not yet and never thought about it to be honest.

32. Looking back, would you do anything differently? If so, please explain. If not, please explain. I am proud of my past.

33. For those of you that want to get married, what qualities do you want in a spouse? Not applicable to me since I am not interested in one.

34. Should a woman who is at least 40 years old, (who dates), be dating for the purpose of getting married? No.

35. How are you living your best life? Building a legacy and focusing on my life goals. Building a legacy and focusing on my life goals.

36. Name some accomplishments, goals, or visions you aspire to complete, have completed, or are working on. Living itself! Right from having been that successful spermatozoa among a million competing ones to fertilize a human ovum, to having managed to live up to the Biblical age of 'three score and ten' (well, almost, touch wood), must in itself die before reaching the age of five, and how utterly unpredictable life in reality is, as though we are playing "Russian Roulette" every moment of our lives, just living is in itself a cause for celebration, and every extended day of one's life must be an added bonus. Life is precious. Enjoy it to the hilt. Carpe Diem.

37. Is there anything else you would like to say on this subject (being a woman who is at least 40 years old, have never been married before, with no children)? Loneliness is about you. I'm not lonely when I'm at the gym even though I'm training by myself, but I am lonely when I go to parties, and I'm a wallflower. Why? Because loneliness is about your engagement in that moment. So, if you're feeling lonely, close your computer and go for a run; it will get you back into the moment.

1. Name: Ayla U.
2. Country: Rwanda
3. City and/or State: Gisenyi
4. Are you happy/satisfied with being single? Yes.
5. Are you happy/satisfied with not having any children? Yes, I am happy/satisfied.

6. Do you or have you ever envied other women who are married and have a child(ren)? No.

7. When you let others know that you have never been married and have no children, what was their response? What was your response to their response? Everyone shares his/her problem with me and say, "So lucky you are not into this" (almost everyone warns me).

8. What have you learned about being single, with no kids? I think when people jump into a relationship the company of a significant other becomes intoxicating. They end up spending loads of time together, so much, that friends and other aspects of their life are usually pushed aside. So, when that person suddenly leaves, breaks up, there is a giant empty hole left behind. That's why it's really important to try and not push friends and hobbies aside for extra time with your significant other. Otherwise, it can leave you feeling really empty and broken when you suddenly find yourself with a bunch of extra alone time. Trust that you're going to want your friends to get through a heartbreak. Don't push them aside. It's a common mistake.

9. What advice do you have for other women 40 and over, who have never been married and never had children? Stop looking for love as something that can be acquired. People always talk about finding or falling in love. Not knowing or realizing that speaking about love in that way first makes it hard to find and second makes it difficult to keep.

10. For those of you that don't ever want to get married or have children, have you encountered any negativity or criticism about this decision? No.

11. Do you have any regrets? No.

12. Do you choose to be single, with no kids, or is it circumstantial? Please explain. I ended up single by choice. Because I wanted to enjoy my life without much responsibility as of now. I don't know how love life is going to be in longer or shorter, but I can't be able to spend quality time for a person. That will become a disappointment to the other one.

13. Have you ever ruined or sabotaged an opportunity to get married/engaged, because of (fear of rejection, commitment, or another reason)? No.

14. If your answer is "Yes" above please explain. No.

15. Do you feel pressured to get married and have a family from outside sources (ex., family, church, friends, society, etc.)? No.

16. Have you ever felt embarrassed about being over 40 and never been married and no kids? No.

17. Have you had a conversation with God about your situation? No.

18. How do you feel about waiting on God to send you the right husband? N/A

19. Do you believe you would have already been married by now? Why? How? If I had my goal focused on having a family by 40, then I could have nurtured a relationship that could have perhaps allowed me to achieve this by the time I hit 40.

20. Are you okay if you never get married and have children? Do you accept this? Are you content? Why? Yes.

21. What advice or words of wisdom would you give to other women in general (whether single or not, with kids or not)? Prepare for your own retirement. In addition to contributing to a retirement savings account, independently or with a life partner, acquire a passive income stream to continue to make money while you're retired.

22. Have you ever been tempted to get married or have a child because you got tired of waiting and you felt time was running out? Give examples. No.

23. Have you been engaged or thought you were going to get married and realized it was going to be a big mistake? What happened? No.

24. Give examples of how you respond to people who question you as to why you're not married? Yes, I am single, but I'm not looking for a relationship/marriage at this time.

25. Have you ever thought about what it would be like to be married with children? Fun, I know.

26. Have you ever sabotaged a relationship/dating because you were afraid of getting married/commitment? If so, explain. No.

27. Are you afraid of getting married? If so, why or for what reason(s)? If not, why or for what reason? Marriage is not my type of thing.

28. Have you been in a position where you were in a relationship or engaged to please others, even though, you knew in your heart that was not the right person for you? No.

29. Have you considered adopting a child(ren), foster care, or some other means, if you never give birth to any child(ren) of your own? If so, what option did you consider and why? Not any.

30. Do you need healing or to come to terms with some pain(s) from the past before you can be open to getting married? No.

31. Have you ever tried online dating to find a mate? If so, what was that experience like? Never.

32. Looking back, would you do anything differently? If so, please explain. If not, please explain. Nothing I could change. I have a great past and I could live over again and again.

33. For those of you that want to get married, what qualities do you want in a spouse? Not interested in marrying.

34. Should a woman who is at least 40 years old, (who dates), be dating for the purpose of getting married? No.

35. How are you living your best life? Vacations and taking care of my body.

36. Name some accomplishments, goals, or visions you aspire to complete, have completed, or are working on. Traveling 100 countries by the time I hit 45.

37. Is there anything else you would like to say on this subject (being a woman who is at least 40 years old, have never been married before, with no children)? Not really.

1. Name: Kehlani P.
2. Country: Benin
3. City and/or State: Porto-Novo
4. Are you happy/satisfied with being single? Maybe.
5. Are you happy/satisfied with not having any children? Not happy/satisfied.
6. Do you or have you ever envied other women who are married and have a child(ren)? Yes.
7. When you let others know that you have never been married and have no children, what was their response? What was your response to their response? My friends make fun of me and say I am self-centered.
8. What have you learned about being single, with no kids? Being single is a gift! Actually, it's the new cool. You hardly see single guys these days.
9. What advice do you have for other women 40 and over, who have never been married and never had children? Live with hobby! Give that hobby all your free time! Start a channel and teach people that hobby! That's the easiest way to be single! Prefer your hobby over people each time you have to choose between these two options!
10. For those of you that don't ever want to get married or have children, have you encountered any negativity or criticism about this decision? Yes.
11. Do you have any regrets? Yes.
12. Do you choose to be single, with no kids, or is it circumstantial? Please explain. Kind of both. For some parts of my life, I was just too busy dealing with life-things to bother. For some parts of my life, I was in hot pursuit of anyone that would give me the time of day, and often ended up alone anyways (this isn't meaning I was desperate, just much more sociable, and open to meeting new people). For some parts of my life, I just wanted to be alone. For

some parts of my life, I wanted to be with someone and wanted to stay with that someone. For some parts of my life, I was with someone and waiting for the perfect time to cut it all off. Today, I'm single mainly because I went through a lot of life changes. I'm currently doing okay and dipping my toes into the dating game, but I haven't had any real luck lately.

13. Have you ever ruined or sabotaged an opportunity to get married/engaged, because of (fear of rejection, commitment, or another reason)? Yes.

14. If your answer is "Yes" above please explain. I met someone online and it turned to be fake person and not the one portrayed online.

15. Do you feel pressured to get married and have a family from outside sources (ex., family, church, friends, society, etc.)? Yes.

16. Have you ever felt embarrassed about being over 40 and never been married and no kids? Yes.

17. Have you had a conversation with God about your situation? Yes.

18. How do you feel about waiting on God to send you the right husband? I pray every day for God to lead me to the right person and I believe He will not fail me.

19. Do you believe you would have already been married by now? Why? How? Yes, if I met a compatible person.

20. Are you okay if you never get married and have children? Do you accept this? Are you content? Why? No no no!

21. What advice or words of wisdom would you give to other women in general (whether single or not, with kids or not)? Women should work hard for their money and not take marriage as a career. Money is sweet when it is your own and you have truly worked hard for it on your own.

22. Have you ever been tempted to get married or have a child because you got tired of waiting and you felt time was running out? Give examples. No.

23. Have you been engaged or thought you were going to get married and realized it was going to be a big mistake? What happened? Yes, I met a pretender online and later realized he was

not going to be a good it for me and I decided to call it quit in the relationship since I felt cheated and betrayed by that person.

24. Give examples of how you respond to people who question you as to why you're not married? I usually give a short answer-because I don't think I could combine the demands of being in a relationship with those of my professional life, and other things I find meaningful.

25. Have you ever thought about what it would be like to be married with children? I believe it would be amazing. I normally have thoughts perhaps of having my first baby in a hospital bed and the nurse handing over the little born child to me to take care.

26. Have you ever sabotaged a relationship/dating because you were afraid of getting married/commitment? If so, explain. No.

27. Are you afraid of getting married? If so, why or for what reason(s)? If not, why or for what reason? Not afraid.

28. Have you been in a position where you were in a relationship or engaged to please others, even though, you knew in your heart that was not the right person for you? No.

29. Have you considered adopting a child(ren), foster care, or some other means, if you never give birth to any child(ren) of your own? If so, what option did you consider and why? Foster care maybe.

30. Do you need healing or to come to terms with some pain(s) from the past before you can be open to getting married? No.

31. Have you ever tried online dating to find a mate? If so, what was that experience like? Yes, and met a guy who was not what I expected and had to end our relationship because of that as stated previously.

32. Looking back, would you do anything differently? If so, please explain. If not, please explain. Perhaps I would not have used dating sites as you do not get a chance to vet a person properly. Nowadays I prefer socializing with friends of friends.

33. For those of you that want to get married, what qualities do you want in a spouse? Openness. The ideal partner is open, undefended, and willing to be vulnerable.

34. Should a woman who is at least 40 years old, (who dates), be dating for the purpose of getting married? Yes.

35. How are you living your best life? I love golf and most of the time that is what I do outside work.

36. Name some accomplishments, goals, or visions you aspire to complete, have completed, or are working on. I aspire to start a blog site on the same topic. The survey questions have been an eye opener about this.

37. Is there anything else you would like to say on this subject (being a woman who is at least 40 years old, have never been married before, with no children)? There is need to respect other people's way of life and how they choose to live it.

1. Name
Nayeli B.
2. Country
Kenya
3. City and/or State
Kisumu
4. Are you happy/satisfied with being single? No.
5. Are you happy/satisfied with not having any children? Not happy/satisfied.
6. Do you or have you ever envied other women who are married and have a child(ren)? Sometimes.
7. When you let others know that you have never been married and have no children, what was their response? What was your response to their response? I do not care how they react.
8. What have you learned about being single, with no kids? I'm sure most parents who have already had children would agree that any disadvantages would not outweigh the benefits but there are benefits to remaining childfree whether that is a choice or not.
9. What advice do you have for other women 40 and over, who have never been married and never had children? That do not feel as you are incomplete in life. Children are not a way to happiness always. There are numerous problems attached to them. Never ever think that those who have children are happier than you. They have their own problems.
10. For those of you that don't ever want to get married or have children, have you encountered any negativity or criticism about this decision? Yes.
11. Do you have any regrets? Yes.
12. Do you choose to be single, with no kids, or is it circumstantial? Please explain. I want to be single forever because I don't need a relationship to be happy and I don't want to waste my time and money that I can't get back doing things I don't want to do. If

you enjoy your freedom and you don't like wasting your time and money on people that don't deserve.

13. Have you ever ruined or sabotaged an opportunity to get married/engaged, because of (fear of rejection, commitment, or another reason)? No.

14. If your answer is "Yes" above please explain. No.

15. Do you feel pressured to get married and have a family from outside sources (ex., family, church, friends, society, etc.)? No.

16. Have you ever felt embarrassed about being over 40 and never been married and no kids? Yes.

17. Have you had a conversation with God about your situation? No.

18. How do you feel about waiting on God to send you the right husband? I pray to God to direct me to the fine things in life.

19. Do you believe you would have already been married by now? Why? How? No.

20. Are you okay if you never get married and have children? Do you accept this? Are you content? Why? I am prepared for anything.

21. What advice or words of wisdom would you give to other women in general (whether single or not, with kids or not)? Not to please people and always speak what is in their minds.

22. Have you ever been tempted to get married or have a child because you got tired of waiting and you felt time was running out? Give examples. No.

23. Have you been engaged or thought you were going to get married and realized it was going to be a big mistake? What happened? No.

24. Give examples of how you respond to people who question you as to why you're not married? I ask them just not to bother me.

25. Have you ever thought about what it would be like to be married with children? I normally think about it, and I believe it is fantastic if you have prepared.

26. Have you ever sabotaged a relationship/dating because you were afraid of getting married/commitment? If so, explain. No.

27. Are you afraid of getting married? If so, why or for what reason(s)? If not, why or for what reason? Yes, I am afraid. Marriage can prevent me from actualizing my many goals in life.
28. Have you been in a position where you were in a relationship or engaged to please others, even though, you knew in your heart that was not the right person for you? No.
29. Have you considered adopting a child(ren), foster care, or some other means, if you never give birth to any child(ren) of your own? If so, what option did you consider and why? Adoption.
30. Do you need healing or to come to terms with some pain(s) from the past before you can be open to getting married? Maybe.
31. Have you ever tried online dating to find a mate? If so, what was that experience like? Yes, once and it wasn't pleasant. I do not like paid sites though.
32. Looking back, would you do anything differently? If so, please explain. If not, please explain. Attend social gatherings often.
33. For those of you that want to get married, what qualities do you want in a spouse? Loving, open minded and honest.
34. Should a woman who is at least 40 years old, (who dates), be dating for the purpose of getting married? Yes.
35. How are you living your best life? Most of the time, I am busy at my business empire.
36. Name some accomplishments, goals, or visions you aspire to complete, have completed, or are working on. Started my own photo studio.
37. Is there anything else you would like to say on this subject (being a woman who is at least 40 years old, have never been married before, with no children)? I think it's wonderful. To see a child grow up to their full potential is a glorious thing if you do it right.

1. Name: Helga O.
2. Country: Austria
3. City and/or State: Vienna
4. Are you happy/satisfied with being single? Maybe.
5. Are you happy/satisfied with not having any children? Not happy/satisfied.
6. Do you or have you ever envied other women who are married and have a child(ren)? Yes.
7. When you let others know that you have never been married and have no children, what was their response? What was your response to their response? I normally invoke comedy most of the time when I tell them, my famous line is that I am still single, but I will gladly accept holiday package for two.
8. What have you learned about being single, with no kids? I've learned that the longer you are by yourself, the truer to yourself you become. But the consequence is that you become less compatible with other people. Since you don't have to, you're not used to regularly tuning into other people's frequencies and molding yourself to be more like them in order to get along.
9. What advice do you have for other women 40 and over, who have never been married and never had children? To continue praying and trusting the process they will get someday.
10. For those of you that don't ever want to get married or have children, have you encountered any negativity or criticism about this decision? Yes.
11. Do you have any regrets? Yes.
12. Do you choose to be single, with no kids, or is it circumstantial? Please explain. It is my choice.
13. Have you ever ruined or sabotaged an opportunity to get married/engaged, because of (fear of rejection, commitment, or another reason)? No.
14. If your answer is "Yes" above please explain. N/A

15. Do you feel pressured to get married and have a family from outside sources (ex., family, church, friends, society, etc.)? Yes.
16. Have you ever felt embarrassed about being over 40 and never been married and no kids? No.
17. Have you had a conversation with God about your situation? Yes.
18. How do you feel about waiting on God to send you the right husband? I feel marriage is honorable and God is the one who invented it, so He will do the necessary.
19. Do you believe you would have already been married by now? Why? How? I dreamed of getting married for as long as I can remember. Many boys that I met in school or at summer camps were passed through the potential mate meter in my mind. This was without even going on a single date. That is how much I was geared to looking for and finding my future husband. I didn't date so much in high school because I didn't get asked out. I think most boys were not so self-confident, but there was at least one boy that I really liked and at least one of them did ask me out a couple of times. The ones I liked the most though, didn't like me back in the same way, so my dream of any of them becoming my husband one day never materialized. In hindsight, that is a good thing. They were not bad guys, but there was a better one yet to come. I went on to university after high school and there I started getting asked out a lot. Boys there, or rather young me, were more self-confident. I liked all the young men I dated, but still, I could tell none was the one, so I didn't usually go out more than a couple times with any one of them. After my first year of college, I became a Christian. This turned my whole world upside down. I started to consider settling down with one guy for more than just a week or two. So, I made up my mind to be more serious with just one person. We dated for 14 months, but in my heart, I knew from the start that I would not marry this person. I broke his heart. I should have never dated him beyond the first couple dates for his sake. He deserved better than that. Following that experience I quit dating. I was going to be content as a single person. I was 21, and I was content for about 10 months, kind of.

There was still this deep ache in my soul. I still wanted a husband. On the campus where I attended university there was a Christian group that sometimes organized a coffee house for Christian students. I was a part of the group and attended these occasional events. I remember one time in early November of 1983, where the speaker asked attendees to pray in pairs with the intent of praying for God to answer a desire of one's heart. My partner, R.S., asked me what he should pray. I answered, "That either God would give me a husband or that he would take this desire for a husband away from me." R.S. prayed and a gentle peace came over me. For the next two weeks I was no longer absorbed with thoughts of finding a husband.

20. Are you okay if you never get married and have children? Do you accept this? Are you content? Why? No.

21. What advice or words of wisdom would you give to other women in general (whether single or not, with kids or not)? To do less talking and more of listening.

22. Have you ever been tempted to get married or have a child because you got tired of waiting and you felt time was running out? Give examples. Never.

23. Have you been engaged or thought you were going to get married and realized it was going to be a big mistake? What happened? No.

24. Give examples of how you respond to people who question you as to why you're not married? Why aren't you single?

25. Have you ever thought about what it would be like to be married with children? Entertaining.

26. Have you ever sabotaged a relationship/dating because you were afraid of getting married/commitment? If so, explain. No.

27. Are you afraid of getting married? If so, why or for what reason(s)? If not, why or for what reason? Not afraid provided it is the right person.

28. Have you been in a position where you were in a relationship or engaged to please others, even though, you knew in your heart that was not the right person for you? No.

29. Have you considered adopting a child(ren), foster care, or some other means, if you never give birth to any child(ren) of your own? If so, what option did you consider and why? Adopting.

30. Do you need healing or to come to terms with some pain(s) from the past before you can be open to getting married? No.

31. Have you ever tried online dating to find a mate? If so, what was that experience like? Never.

32. Looking back, would you do anything differently? If so, please explain. If not, please explain. I would have nurtured relationships at college—serious relationships.

33. For those of you that want to get married, what qualities do you want in a spouse? God-fearing is enough.

34. Should a woman who is at least 40 years old, (who dates), be dating for the purpose of getting married? No.

35. How are you living your best life? Singing in church choir and career.

36. Name some accomplishments, goals, or visions you aspire to complete, have completed, or are working on. To see well beyond the limitations of this life in all directions.

37. Is there anything else you would like to say on this subject (being a woman who is at least 40 years old, have never been married before, with no children)? We are fed illusions from birth. We are stumbling around in a thick fog of our own imagination.

1. Name: June Z.
2. Country: Nigeria
3. City and/or State: Lagos State
4. Are you happy/satisfied with being single? Maybe.
5. Are you happy/satisfied with not having any children? Not happy/satisfied.
6. Do you or have you ever envied other women who are married and have a child(ren)? Sometimes.
7. When you let others know that you have never been married and have no children, what was their response? What was your response to their response? God will give you a husband and family. Keep praying…my response is 'thanks'.
8. What have you learned about being single, with no kids? How to be strong and take care of myself without help. Independence is difficult.
9. What advice do you have for other women 40 and over, who have never been married and never had children? Be strong, take care of yourself. Never be intimidated.
10. For those of you that don't ever want to get married or have children, have you encountered any negativity or criticism about this decision? (No answer)
11. Do you have any regrets? Yes.
12. Do you choose to be single, with no kids, or is it circumstantial? Please explain. It wasn't a choice. I was just unlucky with love, I guess. I don't ever want to raise child/children on my own.
13. Have you ever ruined or sabotaged an opportunity to get married/engaged, because of (fear of rejection, commitment, or another reason)? No.
14. If your answer is "Yes" above please explain. N/A
15. Do you feel pressured to get married and have a family from outside sources (ex., family, church, friends, society, etc.)? Yes.

16. Have you ever felt embarrassed about being over 40 and never been married and no kids? Yes.
17. Have you had a conversation with God about your situation? Yes.
18. How do you feel about waiting on God to send you the right husband? Betrayed.
19. Do you believe you would have already been married by now? Why? How? Honestly don't know.
20. Are you okay if you never get married and have children? Do you accept this? Are you content? Why? I will just have to accept it. I'm already programming my mind to be content if it never happens.
21. What advice or words of wisdom would you give to other women in general (whether single or not, with kids or not)? Be strong, as women there's so much we have to deal with. Always learn to forgive yourself, be kind, think before you speak.
22. Have you ever been tempted to get married or have a child because you got tired of waiting and you felt time was running out? Give examples. Yes, polygamy is acceptable in Nigeria. Without saying it directly my family have suggested it. Dating married men who would be happy to have me as a second or third wife. Official or unofficial with the aim of having children.
23. Have you been engaged or thought you were going to get married and realized it was going to be a big mistake? What happened? I was once engaged but he broke it off. He never explained why. Showed up 12 years later to apologize, but never said why.
24. Give examples of how you respond to people who question you as to why you're not married? I keep it short. I haven't meet him yet has always been my response.
25. Have you ever thought about what it would be like to be married with children? Many times.
26. Have you ever sabotaged a relationship/dating because you were afraid of getting married/commitment? If so, explain. No.

27. Are you afraid of getting married? If so, why or for what reason(s)? If not, why or for what reason? When I was young. Now I'm ok.

28. Have you been in a position where you were in a relationship or engaged to please others, even though, you knew in your heart that was not the right person for you? No.

29. Have you considered adopting a child(ren), foster care, or some other means, if you never give birth to any child(ren) of your own? If so, what option did you consider and why? Yes, adoption.

30. Do you need healing or to come to terms with some pain(s) from the past before you can be open to getting married? Yes.

31. Have you ever tried online dating to find a mate? If so, what was that experience like? Looked at a few sites but I just don't trust them. A lot of them are just men looking for hook ups.

32. Looking back, would you do anything differently? If so, please explain. If not, please explain. Yes, I would. I would marry the first person who asked me to marry him even though I didn't love him.

33. For those of you that want to get married, what qualities do you want in a spouse? Hmmmm!!! I don't know anymore. I guess when I meet him, we could talk about that.

34. Should a woman who is at least 40 years old, (who dates), be dating for the purpose of getting married? Yes.

35. How are you living your best life? Lol.... I can't afford to live my best life.

36. Name some accomplishments, goals, or visions you aspire to complete, have completed, or are working on. Got my degrees while living in the UK. Currently working on getting a better job in Nigeria or eventually going back to the UK.

37. Is there anything else you would like to say on this subject (being a woman who is at least 40 years old, have never been married before, with no children)? It can be lonely and depressing.

NOT EVERY WOMAN

1. Name: Kinley D.
2. Country: USA
3. City and/or State: Chicago
4. Are you happy/satisfied with being single? No.
5. Are you happy/satisfied with not having any children? Not happy/satisfied.
6. Do you or have you ever envied other women who are married and have a child(ren)? I do not envy, I rather admire.
7. When you let others know that you have never been married and have no children, what was their response? What was your response to their response? I am tired of being ridiculed honestly speaking.
8. What have you learned about being single, with no kids? I have learned the value of having a plan for your own life and have things working for you in an autopilot manner.
9. What advice do you have for other women 40 and over, who have never been married and never had children? (No answer).
10. For those of you that don't ever want to get married or have children, have you encountered any negativity or criticism about this decision? No.
11. Do you have any regrets? No.
12. Do you choose to be single, with no kids, or is it circumstantial? Please explain. Circumstantial.
13. Have you ever ruined or sabotaged an opportunity to get married/engaged, because of (fear of rejection, commitment, or another reason)? No.
14. If your answer is "Yes" above please explain. N/A
15. Do you feel pressured to get married and have a family from outside sources (ex., family, church, friends, society, etc.)? Maybe.
16. Have you ever felt embarrassed about being over 40 and never been married and no kids? Maybe.

17. Have you had a conversation with God about your situation? Maybe.
18. How do you feel about waiting on God to send you the right husband? Nothing.
19. Do you believe you would have already been married by now? Why? How? Yes, maybe.
20. Are you okay if you never get married and have children? Do you accept this? Are you content? Why? Not sure.
21. What advice or words of wisdom would you give to other women in general (whether single or not, with kids or not)? Never to trust men.
22. Have you ever been tempted to get married or have a child because you got tired of waiting and you felt time was running out? Give examples. Never.
23. Have you been engaged or thought you were going to get married and realized it was going to be a big mistake? What happened? Never.
24. Give examples of how you respond to people who question you as to why you're not married? To stop poking their noses in other people's affairs.
25. Have you ever thought about what it would be like to be married with children? Wonderful.
26. Have you ever sabotaged a relationship/dating because you were afraid of getting married/commitment? If so, explain. No.
27. Are you afraid of getting married? If so, why or for what reason(s)? If not, why or for what reason? Afraid.
28. Have you been in a position where you were in a relationship or engaged to please others, even though, you knew in your heart that was not the right person for you? No.
29. Have you considered adopting a child(ren), foster care, or some other means, if you never give birth to any child(ren) of your own? If so, what option did you consider and why? I have always contemplated foster care.
30. Do you need healing or to come to terms with some pain(s) from the past before you can be open to getting married? Maybe.

31. Have you ever tried online dating to find a mate? If so, what was that experience like? Once. Not so good and found it insecure.
32. Looking back, would you do anything differently? If so, please explain. If not, please explain. Nothing.
33. For those of you that want to get married, what qualities do you want in a spouse? Patience and understanding.
34. Should a woman who is at least 40 years old, (who dates), be dating for the purpose of getting married? Yes.
35. How are you living your best life? Less attention just me and myself and a few friends close to me make life worthwhile.
36. Name some accomplishments, goals, or visions you aspire to complete, have completed, or are working on. Completed my house.
37. Is there anything else you would like to say on this subject (being a woman who is at least 40 years old, have never been married before, with no children)? N/A

1. Name: Aviana L.
2. Country: Spain
3. City and/or State: Madrid
4. Are you happy/satisfied with being single? No.
5. Are you happy/satisfied with not having any children? Not happy/satisfied.
6. Do you or have you ever envied other women who are married and have a child(ren)? Sometimes.
7. When you let others know that you have never been married and have no children, what was their response? What was your response to their response? Sympathy reaction which I do not like at all.
8. What have you learned about being single, with no kids? I have learned that in this life you are responsible for your own success and happiness.

9. What advice do you have for other women 40 and over, who have never been married and never had children? Work hard, lift weight, do your tasks alone, gain knowledge about more and more fields, walk alone with confidence and push our limits. Don't beg for the equality, establish it.

10. For those of you that don't ever want to get married or have children, have you encountered any negativity or criticism about this decision? Maybe.

11. Do you have any regrets? No.

12. Do you choose to be single, with no kids, or is it circumstantial? Please explain. Circumstantial here.

13. Have you ever ruined or sabotaged an opportunity to get married/engaged, because of (fear of rejection, commitment, or another reason)? No.

14. If your answer is "Yes" above please explain. N/A

15. Do you feel pressured to get married and have a family from outside sources (ex., family, church, friends, society, etc.)? Yes.

16. Have you ever felt embarrassed about being over 40 and never been married and no kids? Yes.

17. Have you had a conversation with God about your situation? No.

18. How do you feel about waiting on God to send you the right husband? No.

19. Do you believe you would have already been married by now? Why? How? Yes!!! Marriage is not the ultimate goal of life!! Society creates pressure to get married at a particular age because of the biological clock ticking and then the ultimate goal after marriage is to pop out kids.

20. Are you okay if you never get married and have children? Do you accept this? Are you content? Why? It is ok till 45-50 years of age but later it will kill my mental health.

21. What advice or words of wisdom would you give to other women in general (whether single or not, with kids or not)? Use your common sense when out and about, at parties and with men you don't know or fully, fully trust. Listen, really listen to your

intuition, and always have an exit plan for every sticky situation-romantic or otherwise. Always have Uber or taxi money at hand.

22. Have you ever been tempted to get married or have a child because you got tired of waiting and you felt time was running out? Give examples. No.

23. Have you been engaged or thought you were going to get married and realized it was going to be a big mistake? What happened? No.

24. Give examples of how you respond to people who question you as to why you're not married? Men are nice, but not absolutely necessary.

25. Have you ever thought about what it would be like to be married with children? Amazing life though I understand full of ups and downs.

26. Have you ever sabotaged a relationship/dating because you were afraid of getting married/commitment? If so, explain. No.

27. Are you afraid of getting married? If so, why or for what reason(s)? If not, why or for what reason? I am afraid or not getting married when I am over 50 years as I normally feel it might get more and more lonely.

28. Have you been in a position where you were in a relationship or engaged to please others, even though, you knew in your heart that was not the right person for you? No.

29. Have you considered adopting a child(ren), foster care, or some other means, if you never give birth to any child(ren) of your own? If so, what option did you consider and why? Adopting.

30. Do you need healing or to come to terms with some pain(s) from the past before you can be open to getting married? Yes.

31. Have you ever tried online dating to find a mate? If so, what was that experience like? Never.

32. Looking back, would you do anything differently? If so, please explain. If not, please explain. I try as much as possible to avoid being depressed and avoid such thoughts much of the time.

33. For those of you that want to get married, what qualities do you want in a spouse? Loyalty is key in this age of diseases. People are sick and will not tell you.

34. Should a woman who is at least 40 years old, (who dates), be dating for the purpose of getting married? No.
35. How are you living your best life? Keep trying new things and visiting new places.
36. Name some accomplishments, goals, or visions you aspire to complete, have completed, or are working on. (No answer).
37. Is there anything else you would like to say on this subject (being a woman who is at least 40 years old, have never been married before, with no children)? (No answer).

1. Name: Liddy B.
2. Country: United States
3. City and/or State: Grand Island, New York
4. Are you happy/satisfied with being single? No.
5. Are you happy/satisfied with not having any children? Not happy/satisfied.
6. Do you or have you ever envied other women who are married and have a child(ren)? Yes.
7. When you let others know that you have never been married and have no children, what was their response? What was your response to their response? They are mostly supportive, and I am grateful for that.
8. What have you learned about being single, with no kids? Too much alone time.
9. What advice do you have for other women 40 and over, who have never been married and never had children? Make friends and keep busy and do what makes you happy.
10. For those of you that don't ever want to get married or have children, have you encountered any negativity or criticism about this decision? (No answer)
11. Do you have any regrets? (No answer)

12. Do you choose to be single, with no kids, or is it circumstantial? Please explain. No, I did not choose that lifestyle. It was very much circumstantial.

13. Have you ever ruined or sabotaged an opportunity to get married/engaged, because of (fear of rejection, commitment, or another reason)? Yes.

14. If your answer is "Yes" above please explain. Mostly fear of rejection. I was bullied and told that I was ugly until I was in my late 20's, and I was afraid that no man could love someone as ugly as me. I have since learned that people aren't ugly and those who say "you're ugly" are lying.

15. Do you feel pressured to get married and have a family from outside sources (ex., family, church, friends, society, etc.)? No.

16. Have you ever felt embarrassed about being over 40 and never been married and no kids? Yes.

17. Have you had a conversation with God about your situation? Yes.

18. How do you feel about waiting on God to send you the right husband? God is taking a long time! Can he pick up the pace?

19. Do you believe you would have already been married by now? Why? How? I don't know.

20. Are you okay if you never get married and have children? Do you accept this? Are you content? Why? Not really.

21. What advice or words of wisdom would you give to other women in general (whether single or not, with kids or not)? Be gentle with yourself and with other people. And adopt a pet. You can use your maternal instincts on a nice cat or dog. I am very happy that I decided to adopt my feline furball.

22. Have you ever been tempted to get married or have a child because you got tired of waiting and you felt time was running out? Give examples. Yes.

23. Have you been engaged or thought you were going to get married and realized it was going to be a big mistake? What happened? Yes, was engaged twice. I realized that it would have been a disaster both times. The engagements ended.

24. Give examples of how you respond to people who question you as to why you're not married? I never met the right person.

25. Have you ever thought about what it would be like to be married with children? Yes. I would be a granny by now.

26. Have you ever sabotaged a relationship/dating because you were afraid of getting married/commitment? If so, explain. I don't know.

27. Are you afraid of getting married? If so, why or for what reason(s)? If not, why or for what reason? Yes. I have written several articles about domestic violence and that's pretty frightening. I'd rather be single than an abuse victim.

28. Have you been in a position where you were in a relationship or engaged to please others, even though, you knew in your heart that was not the right person for you? No.

29. Have you considered adopting a child(ren), foster care, or some other means, if you never give birth to any child(ren) of your own? If so, what option did you consider and why? I considered adopting but knew I wasn't financially solid enough to do so.

30. Do you need healing or to come to terms with some pain(s) from the past before you can be open to getting married? Maybe.

31. Have you ever tried online dating to find a mate? If so, what was that experience like? Yes, not successful.

32. Looking back, would you do anything differently? If so, please explain. If not, please explain. Oh, those boys who wanted to go all the way when I was in my early teens. I would have let them. I didn't know that I would never be a mommy.

33. For those of you that want to get married, what qualities do you want in a spouse? Gentle, kind, good sense of humor, a friend for life. Oh, and he has to like cats and dogs! I have a cat. Wouldn't mind adding a dog to the family!

34. Should a woman who is at least 40 years old, (who dates), be dating for the purpose of getting married? Yes.

35. How are you living your best life? Doing art and photography, learning tap dance, singing in a choir, being a journalist.

36. Name some accomplishments, goals, or visions you aspire to complete, have completed, or are working on. I hope to write a novel.

37. Is there anything else you would like to say on this subject (being a woman who is at least 40 years old, have never been married before, with no children)? Life is a good adventure that is best when it's shared!

1. Name: Braelynn G.
2. Country: US
3. City and/or State: Chicago
4. Are you happy/satisfied with being single? No.
5. Are you happy/satisfied with not having any children? Not happy/satisfied.
6. Do you or have you ever envied other women who are married and have a child(ren)? Most of times.
7. When you let others know that you have never been married and have no children, what was their response? What was your response to their response? They want to know the reasons and I tell them nothing but the truth.
8. What have you learned about being single, with no kids? Being single has taught me to plan well for my old age since I maybe all alone in the future.
9. What advice do you have for other women 40 and over, who have never been married and never had children? Not to allow their situation to deter them from accomplishing their goals and aims in life.
10. For those of you that don't ever want to get married or have children, have you encountered any negativity or criticism about this decision? No.
11. Do you have any regrets? No.

12. Do you choose to be single, with no kids, or is it circumstantial? Please explain. It is circumstantial because of things beyond my control.
13. Have you ever ruined or sabotaged an opportunity to get married/engaged, because of (fear of rejection, commitment, or another reason)? No.
14. If your answer is "Yes" above please explain. No.
15. Do you feel pressured to get married and have a family from outside sources (ex., family, church, friends, society, etc.)? No.
16. Have you ever felt embarrassed about being over 40 and never been married and no kids? No.
17. Have you had a conversation with God about your situation? No.
18. How do you feel about waiting on God to send you the right husband? I believe if God decided to send the right husband, then it will eventually work.
19. Do you believe you would have already been married by now? Why? How? Yes, if all went according to God's plan.
20. Are you okay if you never get married and have children? Do you accept this? Are you content? Why? No, since this means when I die, I will be forgotten forever. With children, at least you are remembered.
21. What advice or words of wisdom would you give to other women in general (whether single or not, with kids or not)? I would advise my fellow women to not depend on a man for anything. Even if you are dating you should be mature enough to incur the expenses.
22. Have you ever been tempted to get married or have a child because you got tired of waiting and you felt time was running out? Give examples. No.
23. Have you been engaged or thought you were going to get married and realized it was going to be a big mistake? What happened? No.
24. Give examples of how you respond to people who question you as to why you're not married? Say, "How will it help you?"

25. Have you ever thought about what it would be like to be married with children? Yes.
26. Have you ever sabotaged a relationship/dating because you were afraid of getting married/commitment? If so, explain. No.
27. Are you afraid of getting married? If so, why or for what reason(s)? If not, why or for what reason? I am not afraid of marriage. At my age I am not.
28. Have you been in a position where you were in a relationship or engaged to please others, even though, you knew in your heart that was not the right person for you? Maybe.
29. Have you considered adopting a child(ren), foster care, or some other means, if you never give birth to any child(ren) of your own? If so, what option did you consider and why? Foster.
30. Do you need healing or to come to terms with some pain(s) from the past before you can be open to getting married? Maybe.
31. Have you ever tried online dating to find a mate? If so, what was that experience like? Online dating is a waste of time and full of blind dates.
32. Looking back, would you do anything differently? If so, please explain. If not, please explain. I can't control.
33. For those of you that want to get married, what qualities do you want in a spouse? I want an honest, caring, and loving man.
34. Should a woman who is at least 40 years old, (who dates), be dating for the purpose of getting married? No.
35. How are you living your best life? Taking part in charity activities and helping the needy.
36. Name some accomplishments, goals, or visions you aspire to complete, have completed, or are working on. My goal is to visit Germany before the year ends.
37. Is there anything else you would like to say on this subject (being a woman who is at least 40 years old, have never been married before, with no children)? We women in this group go through a lot of ridicule. It is very crucial if you can raise a voice to protect us.

1. Name: April E.
2. Country: US
3. City and/or State: Florida
4. Are you happy/satisfied with being single? Yes.
5. Are you happy/satisfied with not having any children? Yes, I am happy/satisfied.
6. Do you or have you ever envied other women who are married and have a child(ren)? No.
7. When you let others know that you have never been married and have no children, what was their response? What was your response to their response? I tell others I am living my best life and instead request then to share with me their expectations in their marriage life.
8. What have you learned about being single, with no kids? You are 100% responsible for your failures and how to overcome them.
9. What advice do you have for other women 40 and over, who have never been married and never had children? Not having children at 40 is not the end of the world for them.
10. For those of you that don't ever want to get married or have children, have you encountered any negativity or criticism about this decision? Maybe.
11. Do you have any regrets? No.
12. Do you choose to be single, with no kids, or is it circumstantial? Please explain. I choose to be single since I love doing my stuff all alone.
13. Have you ever ruined or sabotaged an opportunity to get married/engaged, because of (fear of rejection, commitment, or another reason)? No.
14. If your answer is "Yes" above please explain. N/A
15. Do you feel pressured to get married and have a family from outside sources (ex., family, church, friends, society, etc.)? No.

16. Have you ever felt embarrassed about being over 40 and never been married and no kids? Maybe.
17. Have you had a conversation with God about your situation? Yes.
18. How do you feel about waiting on God to send you the right husband? Not waiting. I ask God for other things.
19. Do you believe you would have already been married by now? Why? How? No, I have never set myself out there looking for relationship or marriage.
20. Are you okay if you never get married and have children? Do you accept this? Are you content? Why? Yes.
21. What advice or words of wisdom would you give to other women in general (whether single or not, with kids or not)? Not to despair in their endeavors.
22. Have you ever been tempted to get married or have a child because you got tired of waiting and you felt time was running out? Give examples. No. Children have not been my thought.
23. Have you been engaged or thought you were going to get married and realized it was going to be a big mistake? What happened? Never.
24. Give examples of how you respond to people who question you as to why you're not married? I will marry when I want.
25. Have you ever thought about what it would be like to be married with children? Never.
26. Have you ever sabotaged a relationship/dating because you were afraid of getting married/commitment? If so, explain. No.
27. Are you afraid of getting married? If so, why or for what reason(s)? If not, why or for what reason? I am afraid of marriage because I do not want commitments.
28. Have you been in a position where you were in a relationship or engaged to please others, even though, you knew in your heart that was not the right person for you? No.
29. Have you considered adopting a child(ren), foster care, or some other means, if you never give birth to any child(ren) of your own? If so, what option did you consider and why? Adoption maybe.

30. Do you need healing or to come to terms with some pain(s) from the past before you can be open to getting married? Maybe.
31. Have you ever tried online dating to find a mate? If so, what was that experience like? Yes, and it backfired.
32. Looking back, would you do anything differently? If so, please explain. If not, please explain. No.
33. For those of you that want to get married, what qualities do you want in a spouse? Not interested.
34. Should a woman who is at least 40 years old, (who dates), be dating for the purpose of getting married? No.
35. How are you living your best life? Work. Work. Work. Fun, Fun.
36. Name some accomplishments, goals, or visions you aspire to complete, have completed, or are working on. My vision is to build a business that will have global outreach or be in every country.
37. Is there anything else you would like to say on this subject (being a woman who is at least 40 years old, have never been married before, with no children)? We should exercise patience and be prepared for the best while expecting for the worst as at 40 getting married is a 40-60%.

1. Name: Colette G.
2. Country: USA
3. City and/or State: Philadelphia
4. Are you happy/satisfied with being single? Maybe.
5. Are you happy/satisfied with not having any children? Not happy/satisfied.
6. Do you or have you ever envied other women who are married and have a child(ren)? No.
7. When you let others know that you have never been married and have no children, what was their response? What was your response to their response? Most are concerned and I explain to them why I choose to remain single.
8. What have you learned about being single, with no kids? Kids are awesome, family is awesome, but there are times when you have to make decisions that is neither popular in order to go far.
9. What advice do you have for other women 40 and over, who have never been married and never had children? Not listen to societal voices or expectations and make decisions they will regret.
10. For those of you that don't ever want to get married or have children, have you encountered any negativity or criticism about this decision? No.
11. Do you have any regrets? No.
12. Do you choose to be single, with no kids, or is it circumstantial? Please explain. Single by choice and I have no regrets.
13. Have you ever ruined or sabotaged an opportunity to get married/engaged, because of (fear of rejection, commitment, or another reason)? No.
14. If your answer is "Yes" above please explain. N/A
15. Do you feel pressured to get married and have a family from outside sources (ex., family, church, friends, society, etc.)? No.
16. Have you ever felt embarrassed about being over 40 and never been married and no kids? No.

17. Have you had a conversation with God about your situation? No.
18. How do you feel about waiting on God to send you the right husband? Nothing.
19. Do you believe you would have already been married by now? Why? How? Yes, if I wanted to get married, I believe I would have done so in my late 20's.
20. Are you okay if you never get married and have children? Do you accept this? Are you content? Why? Yes, I accept.
21. What advice or words of wisdom would you give to other women in general (whether single or not, with kids or not)? Do not look at the spec in another person's eye before removing the spec in your own eyes.
22. Have you ever been tempted to get married or have a child because you got tired of waiting and you felt time was running out? Give examples. No.
23. Have you been engaged or thought you were going to get married and realized it was going to be a big mistake? What happened? Never.
24. Give examples of how you respond to people who question you as to why you're not married? I tell them to keep off from my private life.
25. Have you ever thought about what it would be like to be married with children? Not really.
26. Have you ever sabotaged a relationship/dating because you were afraid of getting married/commitment? If so, explain. No.
27. Are you afraid of getting married? If so, why or for what reason(s)? If not, why or for what reason? I am afraid getting married will detract me from accomplishing things I have planned for.
28. Have you been in a position where you were in a relationship or engaged to please others, even though, you knew in your heart that was not the right person for you? Yes.
29. Have you considered adopting a child(ren), foster care, or some other means, if you never give birth to any child(ren) of

your own? If so, what option did you consider and why? With dreams of venturing into politics, all are okay.

30. Do you need healing or to come to terms with some pain(s) from the past before you can be open to getting married? No.

31. Have you ever tried online dating to find a mate? If so, what was that experience like? Yes, when I was in high school. Most of the time, it was for fun and nothing serious.

32. Looking back, would you do anything differently? If so, please explain. If not, please explain. I would have gone for friendship with benefits and co-parenting.

33. For those of you that want to get married, what qualities do you want in a spouse? N/A

34. Should a woman who is at least 40 years old, (who dates), be dating for the purpose of getting married? No.

35. How are you living your best life? Transforming lives of the less fortunate and helping the vulnerable members of the society.

36. Name some accomplishments, goals, or visions you aspire to complete, have completed, or are working on. I aspire to view for a Congress position in next election.

37. Is there anything else you would like to say on this subject (being a woman who is at least 40 years old, have never been married before, with no children)? Not now.

1. Name: Dorothy W.
2. Country: USA
3. City and/or State: Washington
4. Are you happy/satisfied with being single? Maybe.
5. Are you happy/satisfied with not having any children? Not happy/satisfied.
6. Do you or have you ever envied other women who are married and have a child(ren)? Never.
7. When you let others know that you have never been married and have no children, what was their response? What was your response to their response? They make jokes at me, and I end up being embarrassed mostly because of this.
8. What have you learned about being single, with no kids? I'd say I think about being single every day, regardless of my mood, or what's going on. It's just more some days than others.
9. What advice do you have for other women 40 and over, who have never been married and never had children? To have time to focus on oneself and not to worry about anything else.
10. For those of you that don't ever want to get married or have children, have you encountered any negativity or criticism about this decision? Yes.
11. Do you have any regrets? Maybe.
12. Do you choose to be single, with no kids, or is it circumstantial? Please explain. I am single because of circumstances. I developed a serious illness making me undesirable by others.
13. Have you ever ruined or sabotaged an opportunity to get married/engaged, because of (fear of rejection, commitment, or another reason)? No.
14. If your answer is "Yes" above please explain. N/A
15. Do you feel pressured to get married and have a family from outside sources (ex., family, church, friends, society, etc.)? No.

16. Have you ever felt embarrassed about being over 40 and never been married and no kids? Yes.
17. Have you had a conversation with God about your situation? Yes.
18. How do you feel about waiting on God to send you the right husband? I just pray for God's healing on my condition.
19. Do you believe you would have already been married by now? Why? How? Yes, I believe so in the event there was no disease involved.
20. Are you okay if you never get married and have children? Do you accept this? Are you content? Why? It will be hurtful to me.
21. What advice or words of wisdom would you give to other women in general (whether single or not, with kids or not)? People should not judge why single people are single before knowing their story.
22. Have you ever been tempted to get married or have a child because you got tired of waiting and you felt time was running out? Give examples. No.
23. Have you been engaged or thought you were going to get married and realized it was going to be a big mistake? What happened? Yes, I was engaged to some guy. In fact, he was the one who realized it was going to be a big mistake hence he was the one who abandoned me. He left and disappeared. I have never seen him. I know he is not dead, but just ran away.
24. Give examples of how you respond to people who question you as to why you're not married? I never really talk to anyone about what I think about not being in a relationship/marriage.
25. Have you ever thought about what it would be like to be married with children? I would also have loved to be called a mom someday.
26. Have you ever sabotaged a relationship/dating because you were afraid of getting married/commitment? If so, explain. My relationship was in fact sabotaged.
27. Are you afraid of getting married? If so, why or for what reason(s)? If not, why or for what reason? I am afraid of the fact

that because of my sickness and condition even if I were to get married it will not work.

28. Have you been in a position where you were in a relationship or engaged to please others, even though, you knew in your heart that was not the right person for you? No.

29. Have you considered adopting a child(ren), foster care, or some other means, if you never give birth to any child(ren) of your own? If so, what option did you consider and why? Foster care is fine with me.

30. Do you need healing or to come to terms with some pain(s) from the past before you can be open to getting married? Yes.

31. Have you ever tried online dating to find a mate? If so, what was that experience like? I haven't given it a try yet.

32. Looking back, would you do anything differently? If so, please explain. If not, please explain. I don't think there is anything I could change from the past.

33. For those of you that want to get married, what qualities do you want in a spouse? I want a husband who will accept me in health and sickness with my condition.

34. Should a woman who is at least 40 years old, (who dates), be dating for the purpose of getting married? No.

35. How are you living your best life? Reading the Bible and praying every day to God.

36. Name some accomplishments, goals, or visions you aspire to complete, have completed, or are working on. Became a Sunday School teacher recently and I interact with the children as mine.

37. Is there anything else you would like to say on this subject (being a woman who is at least 40 years old, have never been married before, with no children)? Just a word of advice…do unto others what you would want to be done unto you.

1. Name: Isabella A.
2. Country: France
3. City and/or State: Marseille
4. Are you happy/satisfied with being single? Yes.
5. Are you happy/satisfied with not having any children? Yes, I am happy/satisfied.
6. Do you or have you ever envied other women who are married and have a child(ren)? No.
7. When you let others know that you have never been married and have no children, what was their response? What was your response to their response? I am asked to explain why, and I give finer details.
8. What have you learned about being single, with no kids? I have learned that being single is a state of mind as there are many people available in the market right now and you can have one for yourself easily.
9. What advice do you have for other women 40 and over, who have never been married and never had children? Never get married. Go on vacation when and where you want.
10. For those of you that don't ever want to get married or have children, have you encountered any negativity or criticism about this decision? No.
11. Do you have any regrets? No.
12. Do you choose to be single, with no kids, or is it circumstantial? Please explain. My personal decision is to be single and not changing anytime soon.
13. Have you ever ruined or sabotaged an opportunity to get married/engaged, because of (fear of rejection, commitment, or another reason)?
No, not yet ruined or sabotaged an opportunity but I know if it presented itself, I will ruin it.
14. If your answer is "Yes" above please explain. N/A

15. Do you feel pressured to get married and have a family from outside sources (ex., family, church, friends, society, etc.)? Maybe.
16. Have you ever felt embarrassed about being over 40 and never been married and no kids? No.
17. Have you had a conversation with God about your situation? Maybe.
18. How do you feel about waiting on God to send you the right husband? God has three responses when we pray: No, Yes, and Wait. I normally feel mine was a no and I accepted it.
19. Do you believe you would have already been married by now? Why? How? I don't think so.
20. Are you okay if you never get married and have children? Do you accept this? Are you content? Why? Yes.
21. What advice or words of wisdom would you give to other women in general (whether single or not, with kids or not)? Don't be afraid to ask for what you want.
22. Have you ever been tempted to get married or have a child because you got tired of waiting and you felt time was running out? Give examples. Never.
23. Have you been engaged or thought you were going to get married and realized it was going to be a big mistake? What happened? No.
24. Give examples of how you respond to people who question you as to why you're not married? To stop poking their noses.
25. Have you ever thought about what it would be like to be married with children? Exciting, but I also think a time snatcher.
26. Have you ever sabotaged a relationship/dating because you were afraid of getting married/commitment? If so, explain. No.
27. Are you afraid of getting married? If so, why or for what reason(s)? If not, why or for what reason? Not afraid.
28. Have you been in a position where you were in a relationship or engaged to please others, even though, you knew in your heart that was not the right person for you? No.
29. Have you considered adopting a child(ren), foster care, or some other means, if you never give birth to any child(ren) of your own? If so, what option did you consider and why? Adopting.

30. Do you need healing or to come to terms with some pain(s) from the past before you can be open to getting married? Yes.

31. Have you ever tried online dating to find a mate? If so, what was that experience like? Yes, and I met three guys from there for a date.

32. Looking back, would you do anything differently? If so, please explain. If not, please explain. Tried much of online dating because it was fun.

33. For those of you that want to get married, what qualities do you want in a spouse? I am okay.

34. Should a woman who is at least 40 years old, (who dates), be dating for the purpose of getting married? Yes.

35. How are you living your best life? I avoid the news as much as possible.

36. Name some accomplishments, goals, or visions you aspire to complete, have completed, or are working on. I have met many people, and some have turned out to be wonderful business partners and aided in my growth.

37. Is there anything else you would like to say on this subject (being a woman who is at least 40 years old, have never been married before, with no children)? To all the women in this category, community is one of the most important needs we have. Making a consistent effort to meet new people helps us fulfill that need and introduces us to new ideas and perspectives.

1. Name: Ila F.
2. Country: Wales
3. City and/or State: Cardiff
4. Are you happy/satisfied with being single? Yes.
5. Are you happy/satisfied with not having any children? Not happy/satisfied.
6. Do you or have you ever envied other women who are married and have a child(ren)? Yes.
7. When you let others know that you have never been married and have no children, what was their response? On rare occasions do I but hate talking about it.
8. What have you learned about being single, with no kids? The only person who can heal your old hurts is you.
9. What advice do you have for other women 40 and over, who have never been married and never had children? You can be happy about love and still be single.
10. For those of you that don't ever want to get married or have children, have you encountered any negativity or criticism about this decision? Yes.
11. Do you have any regrets? Maybe.
12. Do you choose to be single, with no kids, or is it circumstantial? I will be honest here: I am single by choice not because I cannot get myself a man.
13. Have you ever ruined or sabotaged an opportunity to get married/engaged, because of (fear of rejection, commitment, or another reason)? No.
14. If your answer is "Yes" above please explain. N/A
15. Do you feel pressured to get married and have a family from outside sources (ex., family, church, friends, society, etc.)? No.
16. Have you ever felt embarrassed about being over 40 and never been married and no kids? No.

17. Have you had a conversation with God about your situation? No.
18. How do you feel about waiting on God to send you the right husband? (No answer).
19. Do you believe you would have already been married by now? Why? How? Yes, I have declined many date invites.
20. Are you okay if you never get married and have children? Do you accept this? Are you content? Why? I'm building a career, I'm developing new skills, I'm processing—I'm doing my own thing without having to adapt myself and my life to someone else's demands and requirements. If you think that's such a sad, lonely existence, you should try it sometime.
21. What advice or words of wisdom would you give to other women in general (whether single or not, with kids or not)? Don't be afraid to be yourself and do everything with grace.
22. Have you ever been tempted to get married or have a child because you got tired of waiting and you felt time was running out? Give examples. No.
23. Have you been engaged or thought you were going to get married and realized it was going to be a big mistake? What happened? Never.
24. Give examples of how you respond to people who question you as to why you're not married? Being single is far better than being with the wrong person.
25. Have you ever thought about what it would be like to be married with children? Don't get me wrong, I don't plan on being single forever, but I reserve my right to be single when I want.
26. Have you ever sabotaged a relationship/dating because you were afraid of getting married/commitment? If so, explain. (No answer)
27. Are you afraid of getting married? If so, why or for what reason(s)? If not, why or for what reason? I'm not undatable, I'm not miserable, and I'm sure am not lonely. Why is it so hard for people to understand that I'm perfectly happy just being on my own?

28. Have you been in a position where you were in a relationship or engaged to please others, even though, you knew in your heart that was not the right person for you? Yes.

29. Have you considered adopting a child(ren), foster care, or some other means, if you never give birth to any child(ren) of your own? If so, what option did you consider and why? Foster care.

30. Do you need healing or to come to terms with some pain(s) from the past before you can be open to getting married? No.

31. Have you ever tried online dating to find a mate? If so, what was that experience like? No, I find it so desperate of a move.

32. Looking back, would you do anything differently? If so, please explain. If not, please explain. No.

33. For those of you that want to get married, what qualities do you want in a spouse? I would prefer to meet a person who is also single like me and we complete each other.

34. Should a woman who is at least 40 years old, (who dates), be dating for the purpose of getting married? No.

35. How are you living your best life? It is happy for me to be happy on my own. Anyway, radical people think you must be in a relationship to be happy.

36. Name some accomplishments, goals, or visions you aspire to complete, have completed, or are working on. I am learning how to bake.

37. Is there anything else you would like to say on this subject (being a woman who is at least 40 years old, have never been married before, with no children)? Finding the right person is a marathon, not a sprint.

1. Name: Emmeline J.
2. Country: US
3. City and/or State: Houston
4. Are you happy/satisfied with being single? No.
5. Are you happy/satisfied with not having any children? Yes, I am happy/satisfied.
6. Do you or have you ever envied other women who are married and have a child(ren)? No.
7. When you let others know that you have never been married and have no children, what was their response? What was your response to their response? They tell me my time will come. I appreciate the vote of confidence, but I hate the feeling that my life is being reduced to something that can be needlepointed onto a pillow.
8. What have you learned about being single, with no kids? It is better to be single than with a clingy and insecure person.
9. What advice do you have for other women 40 and over, who have never been married and never had children? Always speak what is in your mind and follow your heart.
10. For those of you that don't ever want to get married or have children, have you encountered any negativity or criticism about this decision? No.
11. Do you have any regrets? No.
12. Do you choose to be single, with no kids, or is it circumstantial? Please explain. I choose to take my time and figure out my life properly.
13. Have you ever ruined or sabotaged an opportunity to get married/engaged, because of (fear of rejection, commitment, or another reason)? No.
14. If your answer is "Yes" above please explain. N/A
15. Do you feel pressured to get married and have a family from outside sources (ex., family, church, friends, society, etc.)? No.

16. Have you ever felt embarrassed about being over 40 and never been married and no kids? Yes.
17. Have you had a conversation with God about your situation? Maybe.
18. How do you feel about waiting on God to send you the right husband? God is gracious!
19. Do you believe you would have already been married by now? Why? How? (no answer)
20. Are you okay if you never get married and have children? Do you accept this? Are you content? Why? Yes.
21. What advice or words of wisdom would you give to other women in general (whether single or not, with kids or not)? Men are as endless as desires and as many as starts. Their expansion matches with the expansion of universe and their vividness is plethoric. Hence, they can't be listed.
22. Have you ever been tempted to get married or have a child because you got tired of waiting and you felt time was running out? Give examples. Never.
23. Have you been engaged or thought you were going to get married and realized it was going to be a big mistake? What happened? No.
24. Give examples of how you respond to people who question you as to why you're not married? My life just like my dress—it is my choice.
25. Have you ever thought about what it would be like to be married with children? No.
26. Have you ever sabotaged a relationship/dating because you were afraid of getting married/commitment? If so, explain. Never.
27. Are you afraid of getting married? If so, why or for what reason(s)? If not, why or for what reason? I am afraid of being involved in a failed marriage.
28. Have you been in a position where you were in a relationship or engaged to please others, even though, you knew in your heart that was not the right person for you? Yes.
29. Have you considered adopting a child(ren), foster care, or some other means, if you never give birth to any child(ren) of

your own? If so, what option did you consider and why? Both are better choices for me.

30. Do you need healing or to come to terms with some pain(s) from the past before you can be open to getting married? No.

31. Have you ever tried online dating to find a mate? If so, what was that experience like? No.

32. Looking back, would you do anything differently? If so, please explain. If not, please explain. I am satisfied with my past.

33. For those of you that want to get married, what qualities do you want in a spouse? Have the same core values. Open-minded, listens and hears other people's opinions even if they don't agree, seeks out the truth, never takes any beliefs by heart.

34. Should a woman who is at least 40 years old, (who dates), be dating for the purpose of getting married? No.

35. How are you living your best life? Bringing the best version of myself every day at work.

36. Name some accomplishments, goals, or visions you aspire to complete, have completed, or are working on. I am certain that the coming five years will be productive for me. Working in an esteemed organization with a positive work environment can be rewarding. I can picture myself growing to the position I am working on.

37. Is there anything else you would like to say on this subject (being a woman who is at least 40 years old, have never been married before, with no children)? Forty is still young, and many people in their 40's don't know what they want from life and love yet.

1. Name: Marleigh S.
2. Country: Northern Ireland
3. City and/or State: Belfast
4. Are you happy/satisfied with being single? Yes.
5. Are you happy/satisfied with not having any children? Yes, I am happy/satisfied.
6. Do you or have you ever envied other women who are married and have a child(ren)? No.
7. When you let others know that you have never been married and have no children, what was their response? What was your response to their response? Most normally think that I am joking perhaps my husband is abroad.
8. What have you learned about being single, with no kids? Single life is a great time in life to save and invest in yourself.
9. What advice do you have for other women 40 and over, who have never been married and never had children? The forties are tricky to navigate. Though there are inconsequential choices to make, this is also a time with weightier decisions-decisions that can alter the rest of my life.
10. For those of you that don't ever want to get married or have children, have you encountered any negativity or criticism about this decision? Yes.
11. Do you have any regrets? Yes.
12. Do you choose to be single, with no kids, or is it circumstantial? Please explain. Choice.
13. Have you ever ruined or sabotaged an opportunity to get married/engaged, because of (fear of rejection, commitment, or another reason)? Yes.
14. If your answer is "Yes" above please explain. There was this man who was handsome but clingy. I had to end the relationship since he was always insecure and never gave me space. If I told him I was busy, to him it translated I was with another man.

15. Do you feel pressured to get married and have a family from outside sources (ex., family, church, friends, society, etc.)? No.
16. Have you ever felt embarrassed about being over 40 and never been married and no kids? Yes.
17. Have you had a conversation with God about your situation? No.
18. How do you feel about waiting on God to send you the right husband? No.
19. Do you believe you would have already been married by now? Why? How? Sure.
20. Are you okay if you never get married and have children? Do you accept this? Are you content? Why? I am okay.
21. What advice or words of wisdom would you give to other women in general (whether single or not, with kids or not)? Don't carry a grudge. It's way too heavy.
22. Have you ever been tempted to get married or have a child because you got tired of waiting and you felt time was running out? Give examples. Never.
23. Have you been engaged or thought you were going to get married and realized it was going to be a big mistake? What happened? No.
24. Give examples of how you respond to people who question you as to why you're not married? I ignore.
25. Have you ever thought about what it would be like to be married with children? While we adults would like to have a good time, the desire is often tempered by a competing need to get ahead in life or to get things done.
26. Have you ever sabotaged a relationship/dating because you were afraid of getting married/commitment? If so, explain. Never.
27. Are you afraid of getting married? If so, why or for what reason(s)? If not, why or for what reason? No.
28. Have you been in a position where you were in a relationship or engaged to please others, even though, you knew in your heart that was not the right person for you? Maybe.
29. Have you considered adopting a child(ren), foster care, or some other means, if you never give birth to any child(ren) of

your own? If so, what option did you consider and why? Foster care for me.

30. Do you need healing or to come to terms with some pain(s) from the past before you can be open to getting married? No.

31. Have you ever tried online dating to find a mate? If so, what was that experience like? No.

32. Looking back, would you do anything differently? If so, please explain. If not, please explain. Not one thing! Every single shred of "awful, tragic, twisted, beautiful, amazing" from my past is what gave me my present.

33. For those of you that want to get married, what qualities do you want in a spouse? Good looks but humble, strong but caring.

34. Should a woman who is at least 40 years old, (who dates), be dating for the purpose of getting married? Yes.

35. How are you living your best life? Going to the gym and work.

36. Name some accomplishments, goals, or visions you aspire to complete, have completed, or are working on. I am on a weight loss program right now.

37. Is there anything else you would like to say on this subject (being a woman who is at least 40 years old, have never been married before, with no children)? Quality romance to a woman in her 40's is attentiveness and time. We want to feel the connection and want to be wooed through acts of consideration, respect, and support. For us, it's much more romantic and meaningful when a man takes the time to learn how we like their tea rather than to receive flowers.

1. Name: Kinslee N.
2. Country: Scotland
3. City and/or State: Glasgow
4. Are you happy/satisfied with being single? No.
5. Are you happy/satisfied with not having any children? Not happy/satisfied.
6. Do you or have you ever envied other women who are married and have a child(ren)? No.
7. When you let others know that you have never been married and have no children, what was their response? What was your response to their response? (They say) "But you're sooooo great." Then I just acknowledge the compliments.
8. What have you learned about being single, with no kids? Being single is awesome. You can do whatever you want without having to announce it to your significant other.
9. What advice do you have for other women 40 and over, who have never been married and never had children? Never judge either yourself or the other person as right or wrong, good, or bad.
10. For those of you that don't ever want to get married or have children, have you encountered any negativity or criticism about this decision? No.
11. Do you have any regrets? No.
12. Do you choose to be single, with no kids, or is it circumstantial? Please explain. For me it is both.
13. Have you ever ruined or sabotaged an opportunity to get married/engaged, because of (fear of rejection, commitment, or another reason)? No.
14. If your answer is "Yes" above please explain. N/A
15. Do you feel pressured to get married and have a family from outside sources (ex., family, church, friends, society, etc.)? Yes.
16. Have you ever felt embarrassed about being over 40 and never been married and no kids? Yes.

17. Have you had a conversation with God about your situation? No.
18. How do you feel about waiting on God to send you the right husband? No.
19. Do you believe you would have already been married by now? Why? How? Yes.
20. Are you okay if you never get married and have children? Do you accept this? Are you content? Why? Much okay.
21. What advice or words of wisdom would you give to other women in general (whether single or not, with kids or not)? Never play games.
22. Have you ever been tempted to get married or have a child because you got tired of waiting and you felt time was running out? Give examples. Never.
23. Have you been engaged or thought you were going to get married and realized it was going to be a big mistake? What happened? Never.
24. Give examples of how you respond to people who question you as to why you're not married? Ain't nobody got time for that. 80% of your time in a relationship is spent eating pizzas and saying the word "baby" over and over. The rest is wasted in figuring out where to eat. I've got better things to do.
25. Have you ever thought about what it would be like to be married with children? Amazing!
26. Have you ever sabotaged a relationship/dating because you were afraid of getting married/commitment? If so, explain. Yes once, but then I was still an adolescent therefore I think I deserve a benefit of doubt myself.
27. Are you afraid of getting married? If so, why or for what reason(s)? If not, why or for what reason? Yes, I am afraid of the responsibilities that come up with marriage.
28. Have you been in a position where you were in a relationship or engaged to please others, even though, you knew in your heart that was not the right person for you? Yes.
29. Have you considered adopting a child(ren), foster care, or some other means, if you never give birth to any child(ren) of

your own? If so, what option did you consider and why? I prefer foster care.

30. Do you need healing or to come to terms with some pain(s) from the past before you can be open to getting married? Yes.

31. Have you ever tried online dating to find a mate? If so, what was that experience like? I haven't had experience with online dating, but I hear both positive and negative stories from different people.

32. Looking back, would you do anything differently? If so, please explain. If not, please explain. No.

33. For those of you that want to get married, what qualities do you want in a spouse? I want a partner with shared values.

34. Should a woman who is at least 40 years old, (who dates), be dating for the purpose of getting married? No.

35. How are you living your best life? Prioritizing sleep, practicing mindfulness.

36. Name some accomplishments, goals, or visions you aspire to complete, have completed, or are working on. I have served my country in top positions with different responsibilities.

37. Is there anything else you would like to say on this subject (being a woman who is at least 40 years old, have never been married before, with no children)? No.

1. Name: Nita K.
2. Country: Nigeria
3. City and/or State: Kano
4. Are you happy/satisfied with being single? No.
5. Are you happy/satisfied with not having any children? Not happy/satisfied.
6. Do you or have you ever envied other women who are married and have a child(ren)? No.
7. When you let others know that you have never been married and have no children, what was their response? What was your response to their response? Marriage? Sorry I heard pizza. Pizza won't leave you, won't hurt you, won't cheat on you, won't fight with you. Why don't people just marry pizza instead?
8. What have you learned about being single, with no kids? I learned about different things that I can do to lift up my spirit.
9. What advice do you have for other women 40 and over, who have never been married and never had children? Stop wishing what could have been.
10. For those of you that don't ever want to get married or have children, have you encountered any negativity or criticism about this decision? No.
11. Do you have any regrets? No.
12. Do you choose to be single, with no kids, or is it circumstantial? Please explain. By circumstances.
13. Have you ever ruined or sabotaged an opportunity to get married/engaged, because of (fear of rejection, commitment, or another reason)? No.
14. If your answer is "Yes" above please explain. N/A
15. Do you feel pressured to get married and have a family from outside sources (ex., family, church, friends, society, etc.)? Yes.
16. Have you ever felt embarrassed about being over 40 and never been married and no kids? No.

17. Have you had a conversation with God about your situation? No.
18. How do you feel about waiting on God to send you the right husband? N/A
19. Do you believe you would have already been married by now? Why? How? Yes, if I was serious from the start.
20. Are you okay if you never get married and have children? Do you accept this? Are you content? Why? Yes.
21. What advice or words of wisdom would you give to other women in general (whether single or not, with kids or not)? Stop idealizing your ex.
22. Have you ever been tempted to get married or have a child because you got tired of waiting and you felt time was running out? Give examples. No.
23. Have you been engaged or thought you were going to get married and realized it was going to be a big mistake? What happened? Never.
24. Give examples of how you respond to people who question you as to why you're not married? If I wanted drama, I'd watch Bigg Boss!
25. Have you ever thought about what it would be like to be married with children? Yes, quite a lot I think about it.
26. Have you ever sabotaged a relationship/dating because you were afraid of getting married/commitment? If so, explain. Not once, but twice. I have been losing interest so fast.
27. Are you afraid of getting married? If so, why or for what reason(s)? If not, why or for what reason? I am not afraid of getting married. I believe I am an adult to withstand and solve all the challenges that come with marriage.
28. Have you been in a position where you were in a relationship or engaged to please others, even though, you knew in your heart that was not the right person for you? No.
29. Have you considered adopting a child(ren), foster care, or some other means, if you never give birth to any child(ren) of your own? If so, what option did you consider and why? Adopting.

30. Do you need healing or to come to terms with some pain(s) from the past before you can be open to getting married? No.

31. Have you ever tried online dating to find a mate? If so, what was that experience like? I had been on MATCH for about 6 months when I met someone who in no time made me feel like the only woman in the world, so special that I knew in a month he was the one I wanted to spend the rest of my life with. He worked in the military or at least he made me believe he did. I wasn't warned or anything. He was so smooth and loving and naturally, I fell for him. In no time the money request started coming in and I kept on sending like a fool. By the time it occurred to me, I had lost a substantial amount of money I never met. I was distraught and depressed.

32. Looking back, would you do anything differently? If so, please explain. If not, please explain. I focus on my future-that is the only thing within my reach.

33. For those of you that want to get married, what qualities do you want in a spouse? None.

34. Should a woman who is at least 40 years old, (who dates), be dating for the purpose of getting married? Yes.

35. How are you living your best life? Maintaining a happy and healthy life as well as a career.

36. Name some accomplishments, goals, or visions you aspire to complete, have completed, or are working on. Financial stability is what I am aiming at the moment.

37. Is there anything else you would like to say on this subject (being a woman who is at least 40 years old, have never been married before, with no children)? Nothing is more important than family.

1. Name: Zuri F.
2. Country: Australia
3. City and/or State: Perth
4. Are you happy/satisfied with being single? Yes.
5. Are you happy/satisfied with not having any children? Yes, I am happy/satisfied.
6. Do you or have you ever envied other women who are married and have a child(ren)? No.
7. When you let others know that you have never been married and have no children, what was their response? What was your response to their response? They are surprised and I say to them I don't need a partner to prove that I'm worth something.
8. What have you learned about being single, with no kids? There are a lot of great things about being single—a sense of freedom and independence, not being held accountable to a partner, and being able to take a dip into the dating pool.
9. What advice do you have for other women 40 and over, who have never been married and never had children? Rather have a significant income first before thinking of a significant other.
10. For those of you that don't ever want to get married or have children, have you encountered any negativity or criticism about this decision? Yes.
11. Do you have any regrets? No.
12. Do you choose to be single, with no kids, or is it circumstantial? Please explain. I'm fabulous, and I haven't found anyone equally as fabulous, that's why.
13. Have you ever ruined or sabotaged an opportunity to get married/engaged, because of (fear of rejection, commitment, or another reason)? Yes.
14. If your answer is "Yes" above please explain. I have been meeting friends. I mean individuals who are not my type.

15. Do you feel pressured to get married and have a family from outside sources (ex., family, church, friends, society, etc.)? No.

16. Have you ever felt embarrassed about being over 40 and never been married and no kids? Yes.

17. Have you had a conversation with God about your situation? No.

18. How do you feel about waiting on God to send you the right husband? No.

19. Do you believe you would have already been married by now? Why? How? Yes, if I had significant income and also met the right person earlier.

20. Are you okay if you never get married and have children? Do you accept this? Are you content? Why? I will not be okay. I would like to meet a significant person and get married.

21. What advice or words of wisdom would you give to other women in general (whether single or not, with kids or not)? Value yourself before anyone else.

22. Have you ever been tempted to get married or have a child because you got tired of waiting and you felt time was running out? Give examples. No.

23. Have you been engaged or thought you were going to get married and realized it was going to be a big mistake? What happened? No.

24. Give examples of how you respond to people who question you as to why you're not married? I'm not single. I'm married to food.

25. Have you ever thought about what it would be like to be married with children? Yes.

26. Have you ever sabotaged a relationship/dating because you were afraid of getting married/commitment? If so, explain. Yes, for people I met and think they were not compatible with me.

27. Are you afraid of getting married? If so, why or for what reason(s)? If not, why or for what reason? I was never interested in relationships or marriage any point of time since childhood.

28. Have you been in a position where you were in a relationship or engaged to please others, even though, you knew in your heart that was not the right person for you? Yes.

29. Have you considered adopting a child(ren), foster care, or some other means, if you never give birth to any child(ren) of your own? If so, what option did you consider and why? Foster care because it is cheaper than adoption.

30. Do you need healing or to come to terms with some pain(s) from the past before you can be open to getting married? Maybe.

31. Have you ever tried online dating to find a mate? If so, what was that experience like? No.

32. Looking back, would you do anything differently? If so, please explain. If not, please explain. Never.

33. For those of you that want to get married, what qualities do you want in a spouse? Someone who listens to me and is willing to put the work in.

34. Should a woman who is at least 40 years old, (who dates), be dating for the purpose of getting married? No.

35. How are you living your best life? Engaging in fitness and sporting activities.

36. Name some accomplishments, goals, or visions you aspire to complete, have completed, or are working on. I recently learned how to play a violin.

37. Is there anything else you would like to say on this subject (being a woman who is at least 40 years old, have never been married before, with no children)? No.

1. Name: Brooke O.
2. Country: England
3. City and/or State: Bristol
4. Are you happy/satisfied with being single? No.
5. Are you happy/satisfied with not having any children? Not happy/satisfied.
6. Do you or have you ever envied other women who are married and have a child(ren)? No.
7. When you let others know that you have never been married and have no children, what was their response? What was your response to their response? I tell them my breakup story and most of them pity because of the ordeal I went through.
8. What have you learned about being single, with no kids? Cut the negative people from your life too, if necessary, because wrong people can destroy you.
9. What advice do you have for other women 40 and over, who have never been married and never had children? Friendship is a great foundation to a meaningful relationship. Cultivate friendship—maybe you will fall in love someday.
10. For those of you that don't ever want to get married or have children, have you encountered any negativity or criticism about this decision? No.
11. Do you have any regrets? No.
12. Do you choose to be single, with no kids, or is it circumstantial? Please explain. For now, it is by choice. The person I was dating cheated on me, and I don't think I would love to date him again or someone else.
13. Have you ever ruined or sabotaged an opportunity to get married/engaged, because of (fear of rejection, commitment, or another reason)? No.
14. If your answer is "Yes" above please explain. N/A

15. Do you feel pressured to get married and have a family from outside sources (ex., family, church, friends, society, etc.)? Maybe.
16. Have you ever felt embarrassed about being over 40 and never been married and no kids? Maybe.
17. Have you had a conversation with God about your situation? Yes.
18. How do you feel about waiting on God to send you the right husband? I need to be patient when praying and have the belief.
19. Do you believe you would have already been married by now? Why? How? I would have been married for sure, save for betrayal from my partner.
20. Are you okay if you never get married and have children? Do you accept this? Are you content? Why? No.
21. What advice or words of wisdom would you give to other women in general (whether single or not, with kids or not)? Pay attention to the little things. When a man remembers the little details, it can say more than any grand gesture.
22. Have you ever been tempted to get married or have a child because you got tired of waiting and you felt time was running out? Give examples. Never.
23. Have you been engaged or thought you were going to get married and realized it was going to be a big mistake? What happened? No.
24. Give examples of how you respond to people who question you as to why you're not married? I am hurting because of betrayal from a person I saw myself with in the future.
25. Have you ever thought about what it would be like to be married with children? No.
26. Have you ever sabotaged a relationship/dating because you were afraid of getting married/commitment? If so, explain. No. The guy I was once dating is the one who betrayed me. I'm going through betrayal from my boyfriend of the past 6 years. We were the perfect couple who are goals for others! He was head over heels for me and so was I, until one day I found out, he has been cheating on me ever since we are dating. He cheated with multiple people and hid it all way too well. I found it out after 6

years! Not only did I find out his past affairs, but also an affair he was having (at that time).

27. Are you afraid of getting married? If so, why or for what reason(s)? If not, why or for what reason? Not afraid.

28. Have you been in a position where you were in a relationship or engaged to please others, even though, you knew in your heart that was not the right person for you? No.

29. Have you considered adopting a child(ren), foster care, or some other means, if you never give birth to any child(ren) of your own? If so, what option did you consider and why? Adopting is fine.

30. Do you need healing or to come to terms with some pain(s) from the past before you can be open to getting married? No.

31. Have you ever tried online dating to find a mate? If so, what was that experience like? It's the only kind of dating I'll probably ever do. Everyone on a dating site is basically saying: "Hey, I'm available! Talk to me."

32. Looking back, would you do anything differently? If so, please explain. If not, please explain. If I go back to the past and change one thing, then I will not be where I am today. There are regrets, there are mistakes in the past, but I have learned something from them. It made me stronger, though the lessons were harsh. But that's okay. Everything happens for a reason. So, the option of changing the past is ruled out for me.

33. For those of you that want to get married, what qualities do you want in a spouse? A great spouse needs to be polite, respectful, considerate, and attentive to my needs.

34. Should a woman who is at least 40 years old, (who dates), be dating for the purpose of getting married? No.

35. How are you living your best life? Eating nourishing food and exercising.

36. Name some accomplishments, goals, or visions you aspire to complete, have completed, or are working on. To have fun in my journey through life and learn from my mistakes.

37. Is there anything else you would like to say on this subject (being a woman who is at least 40 years old, have never been

married before, with no children)? What you should not do: Agreeing to your parent's demands and marrying someone who you don't like. Thinking that you are aging, and all your friends are getting married and end up marrying someone you don't like.

1. Name: Diana I.
2. Country: England
3. City and/or State: Manchester
4. Are you happy/satisfied with being single? Yes.
5. Are you happy/satisfied with not having any children? Yes, I am happy/satisfied.
6. Do you or have you ever envied other women who are married and have a child(ren)? No.
7. When you let others know that you have never been married and have no children, what was their response? What was your response to their response? Majority don't care and that is a plus and makes it easy for me.
8. What have you learned about being single, with no kids? Choices have consequences. What you do while single will determine your relationships in future. If you are used to doing bad things while single, then this might affect you into your relationship.
9. What advice do you have for other women 40 and over, who have never been married and never had children? Fight your lower self as much as you can every day.
10. For those of you that don't ever want to get married or have children, have you encountered any negativity or criticism about this decision? Yes.
11. Do you have any regrets? No.
12. Do you choose to be single, with no kids, or is it circumstantial? Please explain. It is because of circumstances in life that I am single.

13. Have you ever ruined or sabotaged an opportunity to get married/engaged, because of (fear of rejection, commitment, or another reason)? No.

14. If your answer is "Yes" above please explain. N/A

15. Do you feel pressured to get married and have a family from outside sources (ex., family, church, friends, society, etc.)? No.

16. Have you ever felt embarrassed about being over 40 and never been married and no kids? No.

17. Have you had a conversation with God about your situation? Yes.

18. How do you feel about waiting on God to send you the right husband? God knows my type and I know good things are on the way.

19. Do you believe you would have already been married by now? Why? How? Yes, I do.

20. Are you okay if you never get married and have children? Do you accept this? Are you content? Why? No.

21. What advice or words of wisdom would you give to other women in general (whether single or not, with kids or not)? You should disregard others' unhelpful (and unsolicited) opinions on your looks.

22. Have you ever been tempted to get married or have a child because you got tired of waiting and you felt time was running out? Give examples. Never.

23. Have you been engaged or thought you were going to get married and realized it was going to be a big mistake? What happened? No.

24. Give examples of how you respond to people who question you as to why you're not married? I can't commit to a dinner reservation, let alone another human being.

25. Have you ever thought about what it would be like to be married with children? Yes.

26. Have you ever sabotaged a relationship/dating because you were afraid of getting married/commitment? If so, explain. No.

27. Are you afraid of getting married? If so, why or for what reason(s)? If not, why or for what reason? Not sure.

28. Have you been in a position where you were in a relationship or engaged to please others, even though, you knew in your heart that was not the right person for you? No.

29. Have you considered adopting a child(ren), foster care, or some other means, if you never give birth to any child(ren) of your own? If so, what option did you consider and why? None. I think that we derive a certain fulfillment and gratification from natural children that we don't get from adopted ones. If you were a great athlete in high school, for example, it would be more gratifying to see your natural son or daughter excel in that way than it would to see an adopted child do so. You would still be very happy for them, but not in the same way.

30. Do you need healing or to come to terms with some pain(s) from the past before you can be open to getting married? No.

31. Have you ever tried online dating to find a mate? If so, what was that experience like? No, but I think will try someday.

32. Looking back, would you do anything differently? If so, please explain. If not, please explain. Nothing.

33. For those of you that want to get married, what qualities do you want in a spouse? Mature, honest and with integrity.

34. Should a woman who is at least 40 years old, (who dates), be dating for the purpose of getting married? No.

35. How are you living your best life? I'm enjoying this time in my life when I get to focus on myself and becoming whole as a person.

36. Name some accomplishments, goals, or visions you aspire to complete, have completed, or are working on. Learned French.

37. Is there anything else you would like to say on this subject (being a woman who is at least 40 years old, have never been married before, with no children)? Introduce your single friends to single male friends. Help each other.

1. Name: Nyla K.
2. Country: Uganda
3. City and/or State: Kampala
4. Are you happy/satisfied with being single? No.
5. Are you happy/satisfied with not having any children? Not happy/satisfied.
6. Do you or have you ever envied other women who are married and have a child(ren)? No.
7. When you let others know that you have never been married and have no children, what was their response? What was your response to their response? We joke about it a lot.
8. What have you learned about being single, with no kids? My happiness starts with me.
9. What advice do you have for other women 40 and over, who have never been married and never had children? I would tell them that they are solely responsible for their life and no one else can help.
10. For those of you that don't ever want to get married or have children, have you encountered any negativity or criticism about this decision? No.
11. Do you have any regrets? No.
12. Do you choose to be single, with no kids, or is it circumstantial? Please explain. It is a choice. I have witnessed a lot of bad things happening in marriages.
13. Have you ever ruined or sabotaged an opportunity to get married/engaged, because of (fear of rejection, commitment, or another reason)? No.
14. If your answer is "Yes" above please explain. N/A
15. Do you feel pressured to get married and have a family from outside sources (ex., family, church, friends, society, etc.)? No.
16. Have you ever felt embarrassed about being over 40 and never been married and no kids? Yes.

17. Have you had a conversation with God about your situation? Yes.
18. How do you feel about waiting on God to send you the right husband? I just pray to God to protect me from marriage dramas in the event I got married.
19. Do you believe you would have already been married by now? Why? How? No.
20. Are you okay if you never get married and have children? Do you accept this? Are you content? Why? Not okay, though.
21. What advice or words of wisdom would you give to other women in general (whether single or not, with kids or not)? Women should stop being jealous about other successful women. They should help each other prosper.
22. Have you ever been tempted to get married or have a child because you got tired of waiting and you felt time was running out? Give examples. I have always been feeling time is running out especially now in my forties.
23. Have you been engaged or thought you were going to get married and realized it was going to be a big mistake? What happened? No.
24. Give examples of how you respond to people who question you as to why you're not married? I prefer we change the topic of discussion.
25. Have you ever thought about what it would be like to be married with children? No.
26. Have you ever sabotaged a relationship/dating because you were afraid of getting married/commitment? If so, explain. No.
27. Are you afraid of getting married? If so, why or for what reason(s)? If not, why or for what reason? Yes, I am afraid of experiencing the bad things married people go through.
28. Have you been in a position where you were in a relationship or engaged to please others, even though, you knew in your heart that was not the right person for you? No.
29. Have you considered adopting a child(ren), foster care, or some other means, if you never give birth to any child(ren) of your own? If so, what option did you consider and why? Foster.

30. Do you need healing or to come to terms with some pain(s) from the past before you can be open to getting married? No.

31. Have you ever tried online dating to find a mate? If so, what was that experience like? No.

32. Looking back, would you do anything differently? If so, please explain. If not, please explain. I would change my perception of marriage.

33. For those of you that want to get married, what qualities do you want in a spouse? Supportive and a gentleman.

34. Should a woman who is at least 40 years old, (who dates), be dating for the purpose of getting married? No.

35. How are you living your best life? I love watching movies in my free time and traveling.

36. Name some accomplishments, goals, or visions you aspire to complete, have completed, or are working on. I have a goal to start and oversee a company.

37. Is there anything else you would like to say on this subject (being a woman who is at least 40 years old, have never been married before, with no children)? No.

1. Name: Evangeline P.
2. Country: US
3. City and/or State: Seattle
4. Are you happy/satisfied with being single? No.
5. Are you happy/satisfied with not having any children? Not happy/satisfied.
6. Do you or have you ever envied other women who are married and have a child(ren)? No.
7. When you let others know that you have never been married and have no children, what was their response? What was your response to their response? I normally tell them if I was in their shoes, I would actually choose to be single again.
8. What have you learned about being single, with no kids? Being lonely hurts, but you always get over it. Each time you move past this feeling of loneliness, you learn your strengths and how to overcome painful feelings.
9. What advice do you have for other women 40 and over, who have never been married and never had children? I will say don't settle on the first thing that comes along. Look at all the different factors that make a relationship work. Are you compatible, or is he just good to look at?
10. For those of you that don't ever want to get married or have children, have you encountered any negativity or criticism about this decision? Yes.
11. Do you have any regrets? Maybe.
12. Do you choose to be single, with no kids, or is it circumstantial? Please explain. I choose to be single because of my own principles.
13. Have you ever ruined or sabotaged an opportunity to get married/engaged, because of (fear of rejection, commitment, or another reason)? Yes.
14. If your answer is "Yes" above please explain. The man I was dating wanted sex by force, I had to end the relationship.

15. Do you feel pressured to get married and have a family from outside sources (ex., family, church, friends, society, etc.)? Yes.

16. Have you ever felt embarrassed about being over 40 and never been married and no kids? No.

17. Have you had a conversation with God about your situation? Yes.

18. How do you feel about waiting on God to send you the right husband? I pray to God to give me an understanding person with whom we have chemistry.

19. Do you believe you would have already been married by now? Why? How? Yes, I would have.

20. Are you okay if you never get married and have children? Do you accept this? Are you content? Why? I am okay and will consider adoption.

21. What advice or words of wisdom would you give to other women in general (whether single or not, with kids or not)? First, dating shouldn't be seen as a big move. Yes, it can be scary putting yourself out there, especially in today's world of online dating, but when you're using the right tools that match you based on your compatibility with others, you're taking part of that scariness out of the equation. If you are still overwhelmed with nerves, or uneasiness when looking to meet "the one", that can be a flag that you're not ready yet.

22. Have you ever been tempted to get married or have a child because you got tired of waiting and you felt time was running out? Give examples. No.

23. Have you been engaged or thought you were going to get married and realized it was going to be a big mistake? What happened? I was engaged but was afraid of losing my virginity. The person I was dating then was too demanding and wanted sex and I was not ready.

24. Give examples of how you respond to people who question you as to why you're not married? No answer.

25. Have you ever thought about what it would be like to be married with children? Yes.

26. Have you ever sabotaged a relationship/dating because you were afraid of getting married/commitment? If so, explain. Yes, as mentioned previously.
27. Are you afraid of getting married? If so, why or for what reason(s)? If not, why or for what reason? Yes.
28. Have you been in a position where you were in a relationship or engaged to please others, even though, you knew in your heart that was not the right person for you? Yes.
29. Have you considered adopting a child(ren), foster care, or some other means, if you never give birth to any child(ren) of your own? If so, what option did you consider and why? I consider adoption.
30. Do you need healing or to come to terms with some pain(s) from the past before you can be open to getting married? No.
31. Have you ever tried online dating to find a mate? If so, what was that experience like? Yes, quite a few actually. Believe it or not, I've obtained roughly equal results from both Tinder and OkCupid. I've met great people to simply hang out with, great people to date, and great people to simply realize what I don't want to associate myself with. I have been catfished once, but that situation was due to my fault.
32. Looking back, would you do anything differently? If so, please explain. If not, please explain. I missed the opportunity to be a doctor – my mother always wanted me to be a doctor.
33. For those of you that want to get married, what qualities do you want in a spouse? I just want us to have chemistry.
34. Should a woman who is at least 40 years old, (who dates), be dating for the purpose of getting married? Yes.
35. How are you living your best life? I love journaling and relishing the small things.
36. Name some accomplishments, goals, or visions you aspire to complete, have completed, or are working on. Developed and implemented new operation procedure at work that earned me a promotion.
37. Is there anything else you would like to say on this subject (being a woman who is at least 40 years old, have never been

married before, with no children)? There is no right or wrong way to date or not date. Each person is different and has factors that will play into a successful relationship. One thing we see as a great measure of success is how compatible two people are for each other. Going on date after date, especially after getting out of a long-term relationship or being single for what feels like forever – is like a second job.

1. Name: Jane R.
2. Country: USA
3. City and/or State: Boston
4. Are you happy/satisfied with being single?
Maybe.
5. Are you happy/satisfied with not having any children? Not happy/satisfied.
6. Do you or have you ever envied other women who are married and have a child(ren)? No.
7. When you let others know that you have never been married and have no children, what was their response? What was your response to their response? Others want to know why I am not married at 40. My response is I am still focusing on myself and career.
8. What have you learned about being single, with no kids? I have learned a lot of things that make me happy and those that make me sad and how to cope with each situation.
9. What advice do you have for other women 40 and over, who have never been married and never had children? Just to exercise patience. A spouse comes from God.
10. For those of you that don't ever want to get married or have children, have you encountered any negativity or criticism about this decision? No.
11. Do you have any regrets? No.

12. Do you choose to be single, with no kids, or is it circumstantial? Please explain. It is my choice. My job is so demanding being a nurse.

13. Have you ever ruined or sabotaged an opportunity to get married/engaged, because of (fear of rejection, commitment, or another reason)? No.

14. If your answer is "Yes" above please explain. N/A

15. Do you feel pressured to get married and have a family from outside sources (ex., family, church, friends, society, etc.)? No.

16. Have you ever felt embarrassed about being over 40 and never been married and no kids? Maybe.

17. Have you had a conversation with God about your situation? Maybe.

18. How do you feel about waiting on God to send you the right husband? God is the driver of my life.

19. Do you believe you would have already been married by now? Why? How? Yes, if a compatible person came along.

20. Are you okay if you never get married and have children? Do you accept this? Are you content? Why? I will be okay.

21. What advice or words of wisdom would you give to other women in general (whether single or not, with kids or not)? I advise women not to get involved in drugs or alcohol as it is the surest way to distraction.

22. Have you ever been tempted to get married or have a child because you got tired of waiting and you felt time was running out? Give examples. Never.

23. Have you been engaged or thought you were going to get married and realized it was going to be a big mistake? What happened? I haven't been engaged yet in my life.

24. Give examples of how you respond to people who question you as to why you're not married? I just ask them to politely mind their business since there are a lot of other things to discuss.

25. Have you ever thought about what it would be like to be married with children? No.

26. Have you ever sabotaged a relationship/dating because you were afraid of getting married/commitment? If so, explain. I have

not myself, but I have witnessed a close friend of mine sabotage hers.

27. Are you afraid of getting married? If so, why or for what reason(s)? If not, why or for what reason? I am afraid my job schedule might badly affect my marriage.

28. Have you been in a position where you were in a relationship or engaged to please others, even though, you knew in your heart that was not the right person for you? No.

29. Have you considered adopting a child(ren), foster care, or some other means, if you never give birth to any child(ren) of your own? If so, what option did you consider and why? Both foster care and adoption are great alternatives, but I don't think any can work because of commitments.

30. Do you need healing or to come to terms with some pain(s) from the past before you can be open to getting married? No.

31. Have you ever tried online dating to find a mate? If so, what was that experience like? No.

32. Looking back, would you do anything differently? If so, please explain. If not, please explain. Perhaps I would have gone for a career that is less demanding, who knows I would already be married now.

33. For those of you that want to get married, what qualities do you want in a spouse? Understanding, faithful, and hardworking.

34. Should a woman who is at least 40 years old, (who dates), be dating for the purpose of getting married? No.

35. How are you living your best life? I live my best life by helping in the labor and delivery ward. The joy at the war during delivery is worth it and helping mothers and young parents.

36. Name some accomplishments, goals, or visions you aspire to complete, have completed, or are working on. I aspire to be a fully certified doctor in 3 years' time.

37. Is there anything else you would like to say on this subject (being a woman who is at least 40 years old, have never been married before, with no children)? Women at 40 require time and attention and if by chance marriage works out, most of the

time divorce rates are lower compared to those who get married in their 20's.

1. Name: Lena U.
2. Country: UK
3. City and/or State: Swansea
4. Are you happy/satisfied with being single? Yes.
5. Are you happy/satisfied with not having any children? Yes, I am happy/satisfied.
6. Do you or have you ever envied other women who are married and have a child(ren)? No.
7. When you let others know that you have never been married and have no children, what was their response? What was your response to their response? Most of my friends are over 40 and single too, therefore, it is normally a rare topic of discussion.
8. What have you learned about being single, with no kids? I have learned that birds of the same feathers flock together, most of the people I hang out are also in the same group and normally feel out of place hanging with married people.
9. What advice do you have for other women 40 and over, who have never been married and never had children? Find your niche. Focus on it. It might be your breakthrough.
10. For those of you that don't ever want to get married or have children, have you encountered any negativity or criticism about this decision? No.
11. Do you have any regrets? No.
12. Do you choose to be single, with no kids, or is it circumstantial? Please explain. It is a choice because of my own personal reasons.
13. Have you ever ruined or sabotaged an opportunity to get married/engaged, because of (fear of rejection, commitment, or another reason)? No.
14. If your answer is "Yes" above please explain. N/A

15. Do you feel pressured to get married and have a family from outside sources (ex., family, church, friends, society, etc.)? No.
16. Have you ever felt embarrassed about being over 40 and never been married and no kids? Yes.
17. Have you had a conversation with God about your situation? No.
18. How do you feel about waiting on God to send you the right husband? (No answer)
19. Do you believe you would have already been married by now? Why? How? No. I don't think so honestly.
20. Are you okay if you never get married and have children? Do you accept this? Are you content? Why? Yes.
21. What advice or words of wisdom would you give to other women in general (whether single or not, with kids or not)? Being single is not the end of the world and being married is not a certificate to despise single people.
22. Have you ever been tempted to get married or have a child because you got tired of waiting and you felt time was running out? Give examples. No.
23. Have you been engaged or thought you were going to get married and realized it was going to be a big mistake? What happened? Never.
24. Give examples of how you respond to people who question you as to why you're not married? I tell them I got more pressing issues than getting married and probably ending up being a housewife.
25. Have you ever thought about what it would be like to be married with children? Yes.
26. Have you ever sabotaged a relationship/dating because you were afraid of getting married/commitment? If so, explain. No.
27. Are you afraid of getting married? If so, why or for what reason(s)? If not, why or for what reason? I am afraid of becoming a housewife for sure.
28. Have you been in a position where you were in a relationship or engaged to please others, even though, you knew in your heart that was not the right person for you? Maybe.

29. Have you considered adopting a child(ren), foster care, or some other means, if you never give birth to any child(ren) of your own? If so, what option did you consider and why? Adopting children when I am over 50 years old.

30. Do you need healing or to come to terms with some pain(s) from the past before you can be open to getting married? No.

31. Have you ever tried online dating to find a mate? If so, what was that experience like? Not yet.

32. Looking back, would you do anything differently? If so, please explain. If not, please explain. Looking back, I would have perhaps started a children's home because of the love for children but it is something I am still planning to do.

33. For those of you that want to get married, what qualities do you want in a spouse? None.

34. Should a woman who is at least 40 years old, (who dates), be dating for the purpose of getting married? No.

35. How are you living your best life? Spending time with a group of friends all unmarried and the popular "independent single ladies"; we travel the world and engage in financial support activities to help each other succeed.

36. Name some accomplishments, goals, or visions you aspire to complete, have completed, or are working on. Becoming a millionaire this year. Maybe one day I will be on Forbes list sandwiched among men.

37. Is there anything else you would like to say on this subject (being a woman who is at least 40 years old, have never been married before, with no children)? This is a make-or-break age if you desire to get married. This is the age. Past this age is normally difficult.

1. Name: McKenna V.
2. Country: Canada
3. City and/or State: Ottawa
4. Are you happy/satisfied with being single? No.
5. Are you happy/satisfied with not having any children? Not happy/satisfied.
6. Do you or have you ever envied other women who are married and have a child(ren)? No.
7. When you let others know that you have never been married and have no children, what was their response? What was your response to their response? It's hard not to feel left out when everyone else is paired off, and I am increasingly reluctant to share tales of my current romantic pitfalls with the friends who no longer suffer alongside me, lest they pity or laugh at me when they go home to supportive partners.
8. What have you learned about being single, with no kids? Being single on a prolonged basis is a real form of grief. The life that you're anticipating hasn't come to pass yet.
9. What advice do you have for other women 40 and over, who have never been married and never had children? Don't feel bad for feeling bad about being unmarried.
10. For those of you that don't ever want to get married or have children, have you encountered any negativity or criticism about this decision? Maybe.
11. Do you have any regrets? No.
12. Do you choose to be single, with no kids, or is it circumstantial? Please explain. It is circumstantial but I believe it can be overcome.
13. Have you ever ruined or sabotaged an opportunity to get married/engaged, because of (fear of rejection, commitment, or another reason)? No.
14. If your answer is "Yes" above please explain. N/A

15. Do you feel pressured to get married and have a family from outside sources (ex., family, church, friends, society, etc.)? No.

16. Have you ever felt embarrassed about being over 40 and never been married and no kids? No.

17. Have you had a conversation with God about your situation? Yes.

18. How do you feel about waiting on God to send you the right husband? God knew us before we were even born. I believe God has a plan for everybody.

19. Do you believe you would have already been married by now? Why? How? Yes, I thought I would be married by the time I was 35 years old and fresh from college, but it never came to pass.

20. Are you okay if you never get married and have children? Do you accept this? Are you content? Why? Yes, I would accept.

21. What advice or words of wisdom would you give to other women in general (whether single or not, with kids or not)? The more time you spend isolated from your friends in relationships, the more left out you'll feel.

22. Have you ever been tempted to get married or have a child because you got tired of waiting and you felt time was running out? Give examples. No.

23. Have you been engaged or thought you were going to get married and realized it was going to be a big mistake? What happened? Never.

24. Give examples of how you respond to people who question you as to why you're not married? I feel like I'm the last un-wife holdout, but it turns out there are a lot of me out there.

25. Have you ever thought about what it would be like to be married with children? Yes, amazing!

26. Have you ever sabotaged a relationship/dating because you were afraid of getting married/commitment? If so, explain. No.

27. Are you afraid of getting married? If so, why or for what reason(s)? If not, why or for what reason? Yes, because of the bad marriage stories on the news every day.

28. Have you been in a position where you were in a relationship or engaged to please others, even though, you knew in your heart that was not the right person for you? No.

29. Have you considered adopting a child(ren), foster care, or some other means, if you never give birth to any child(ren) of your own? If so, what option did you consider and why? Adopting is fine.

30. Do you need healing or to come to terms with some pain(s) from the past before you can be open to getting married? No.

31. Have you ever tried online dating to find a mate? If so, what was that experience like? Yes once. Bad experience.

32. Looking back, would you do anything differently? If so, please explain. If not, please explain. No.

33. For those of you that want to get married, what qualities do you want in a spouse? I just want a man with emotional intelligence.

34. Should a woman who is at least 40 years old, (who dates), be dating for the purpose of getting married? No.

35. How are you living your best life? I love coming up with new ideas and every time I try to be innovative, and this makes life worth living.

36. Name some accomplishments, goals, or visions you aspire to complete, have completed, or are working on. Organizing a successful charity event recently.

37. Is there anything else you would like to say on this subject (being a woman who is at least 40 years old, have never been married before, with no children)? Single people too often get ditched by their coupled friends, you should not be that kind or type of friend.

1. Name: Zola A.
2. Country: Tanzania
3. City and/or State: Arusha
4. Are you happy/satisfied with being single? No.
5. Are you happy/satisfied with not having any children? Not happy/satisfied.
6. Do you or have you ever envied other women who are married and have a child(ren)? Sometimes I do feel a bit of envy.
7. When you let others know that you have never been married and have no children, what was their response? What was your response to their response? When I let others know, I feel out of place, but they later accommodate me and things continue as normal or usual.
8. What have you learned about being single, with no kids? I have learned the value friends bring on the table—no person is an island. Some friends are even great than some family members.
9. What advice do you have for other women 40 and over, who have never been married and never had children? I would advise women in this category like me not to lose hope. Good things are coming.
10. For those of you that don't ever want to get married or have children, have you encountered any negativity or criticism about this decision? No.
11. Do you have any regrets? No.
12. Do you choose to be single, with no kids, or is it circumstantial? Please explain. Mine is circumstantial. (I mean traditional or cultural constraints).
13. Have you ever ruined or sabotaged an opportunity to get married/engaged, because of (fear of rejection, commitment, or another reason)? No.
14. If your answer is "Yes" above please explain. N/A

15. Do you feel pressured to get married and have a family from outside sources (ex., family, church, friends, society, etc.)? No.
16. Have you ever felt embarrassed about being over 40 and never been married and no kids? No.
17. Have you had a conversation with God about your situation? Yes.
18. How do you feel about waiting on God to send you the right husband? God will take charge of the situation and lead me through.
19. Do you believe you would have already been married by now? Why? How? Yes, if it were not for traditional constraints in our community.
20. Are you okay if you never get married and have children? Do you accept this? Are you content? Why? Not okay and won't forgive some people.
21. What advice or words of wisdom would you give to other women in general (whether single or not, with kids or not)? Not to stick too much on traditional practices as some are a waste of time.
22. Have you ever been tempted to get married or have a child because you got tired of waiting and you felt time was running out? Give examples. Not really. The pressure is on my elder sister.
23. Have you been engaged or thought you were going to get married and realized it was going to be a big mistake? What happened? Yes, I almost got married but the traditional practices couldn't allow. It is a taboo to get married before the elder sister. She has never been married.
24. Give examples of how you respond to people who question you as to why you're not married? I say as it is, that a lot of things are a hindrance and most want to know what these things are.
25. Have you ever thought about what it would be like to be married with children? Yes, quite often.
26. Have you ever sabotaged a relationship/dating because you were afraid of getting married/commitment? If so, explain. Not really.

27. Are you afraid of getting married? If so, why or for what reason(s)? If not, why or for what reason? I am not afraid but eager to get married one day.

28. Have you been in a position where you were in a relationship or engaged to please others, even though, you knew in your heart that was not the right person for you? No.

29. Have you considered adopting a child(ren), foster care, or some other means, if you never give birth to any child(ren) of your own? If so, what option did you consider and why? Biological children are my prayer.

30. Do you need healing or to come to terms with some pain(s) from the past before you can be open to getting married? No.

31. Have you ever tried online dating to find a mate? If so, what was that experience like? I tried online dating several times but wasn't successful. Most of the people I met on Tinder were after sex and not a serious relationship. I deleted the platform.

32. Looking back, would you do anything differently? If so, please explain. If not, please explain. There is nothing I can change in regard to tradition-that is a great hindrance.

33. For those of you that want to get married, what qualities do you want in a spouse? I want a humble person and a gentleman.

34. Should a woman who is at least 40 years old, (who dates), be dating for the purpose of getting married? No.

35. How are you living your best life? Singing in the church choir and investment.

36. Name some accomplishments, goals, or visions you aspire to complete, have completed, or are working on. Recently beat the sales target at work and awarded a trip to Brazil for two in December.

37. Is there anything else you would like to say on this subject (being a woman who is at least 40 years old, have never been married before, with no children)? No.

1. Name: Lucy B.
2. Country: USA
3. City and/or State: Boston
4. Are you happy/satisfied with being single? Maybe.
5. Are you happy/satisfied with not having any children? Yes, I am happy/satisfied.
6. Do you or have you ever envied other women who are married and have a child(ren)? No.
7. When you let others know that you have never been married and have no children, what was their response? What was your response to their response? I normally feel teased and prefer not taking their jokes too far. People make fun of situations and circumstances they have no control over. Especially when someone else's lifestyle intimidates them in some way.
8. What have you learned about being single, with no kids? I have developed a greater sense of autonomy.
9. What advice do you have for other women 40 and over, who have never been married and never had children? Avoid stress as much as possible and live a stress-free life.
10. For those of you that don't ever want to get married or have children, have you encountered any negativity or criticism about this decision? No.
11. Do you have any regrets? No.
12. Do you choose to be single, with no kids, or is it circumstantial? Please explain. I choose to be single in order to have enough time to pursue my goals in life.
13. Have you ever ruined or sabotaged an opportunity to get married/engaged, because of (fear of rejection, commitment, or another reason)? No.
14. If your answer is "Yes" above please explain. N/A
15. Do you feel pressured to get married and have a family from outside sources (ex., family, church, friends, society, etc.)? No.

16. Have you ever felt embarrassed about being over 40 and never been married and no kids? No.
17. Have you had a conversation with God about your situation? Yes.
18. How do you feel about waiting on God to send you the right husband? God is faithful.
19. Do you believe you would have already been married by now? Why? How? Yes, but there is no way I am going to sacrifice my goals.
20. Are you okay if you never get married and have children? Do you accept this? Are you content? Why? Yes, as long as I achieve my goals.
21. What advice or words of wisdom would you give to other women in general (whether single or not, with kids or not)? Live a stress less life.
22. Have you ever been tempted to get married or have a child because you got tired of waiting and you felt time was running out? Give examples. Never.
23. Have you been engaged or thought you were going to get married and realized it was going to be a big mistake? What happened? No.
24. Give examples of how you respond to people who question you as to why you're not married? To ask about important issues like the economy, fuel prices, and weather.
25. Have you ever thought about what it would be like to be married with children? Yes, it will be exciting.
26. Have you ever sabotaged a relationship/dating because you were afraid of getting married/commitment? If so, explain. Never.
27. Are you afraid of getting married? If so, why or for what reason(s)? If not, why or for what reason? I am afraid of being a failure in life.
28. Have you been in a position where you were in a relationship or engaged to please others, even though, you knew in your heart that was not the right person for you? No.
29. Have you considered adopting a child(ren), foster care, or some other means, if you never give birth to any child(ren) of

your own? If so, what option did you consider and why? Foster care.

30. Do you need healing or to come to terms with some pain(s) from the past before you can be open to getting married? No.

31. Have you ever tried online dating to find a mate? If so, what was that experience like? I find it a waste of time.

32. Looking back, would you do anything differently? If so, please explain. If not, please explain. I would have gotten a child in my 20's, and he/she would be in college.

33. For those of you that want to get married, what qualities do you want in a spouse? Skip for today maybe in the future a hardworking and handsome.

34. Should a woman who is at least 40 years old, (who dates), be dating for the purpose of getting married? No.

35. How are you living your best life? Running business errands and beating sales targets.

36. Name some accomplishments, goals, or visions you aspire to complete, have completed, or are working on. I recently won a global award for entrepreneurship.

37. Is there anything else you would like to say on this subject (being a woman who is at least 40 years old, have never been married before, with no children)? No one should be judgmental.

1. Name: Claire H.
2. Country: USA
3. City and/or State: Austin
4. Are you happy/satisfied with being single? Yes.
5. Are you happy/satisfied with not having any children? Yes, I am happy/satisfied.
6. Do you or have you ever envied other women who are married and have a child(ren)? No, I do not envy.
7. When you let others know that you have never been married and have no children, what was their response? What was your response to their response? I mostly say provided I am living my best life; it is fine, and we have a cheer for that.
8. What have you learned about being single, with no kids? I have enough time for my hobbies and interests.
9. What advice do you have for other women 40 and over, who have never been married and never had children? This is the best era for being single, because when they enter into marriage, they are mature enough.
10. For those of you that don't ever want to get married or have children, have you encountered any negativity or criticism about this decision? No.
11. Do you have any regrets? Maybe.
12. Do you choose to be single, with no kids, or is it circumstantial? Please explain. I choose to be single with no kids.
13. Have you ever ruined or sabotaged an opportunity to get married/engaged, because of (fear of rejection, commitment, or another reason)? No.
14. If your answer is "Yes" above please explain. No.
15. Do you feel pressured to get married and have a family from outside sources (ex., family, church, friends, society, etc.)? Maybe.
16. Have you ever felt embarrassed about being over 40 and never been married and no kids? Yes.

17. Have you had a conversation with God about your situation? No.
18. How do you feel about waiting on God to send you the right husband? I lost hope long ago.
19. Do you believe you would have already been married by now? Why? How? No.
20. Are you okay if you never get married and have children? Do you accept this? Are you content? Why? Yes.
21. What advice or words of wisdom would you give to other women in general (whether single or not, with kids or not)? Work hard and enjoy the results of their hard work.
22. Have you ever been tempted to get married or have a child because you got tired of waiting and you felt time was running out? Give examples. No.
23. Have you been engaged or thought you were going to get married and realized it was going to be a big mistake? What happened? No.
24. Give examples of how you respond to people who question you as to why you're not married? I tell them to their face to stop bothering me.
25. Have you ever thought about what it would be like to be married with children? Yes.
26. Have you ever sabotaged a relationship/dating because you were afraid of getting married/commitment? If so, explain. Never sabotaged any relationship and I don't think I can. I believe in communication.
27. Are you afraid of getting married? If so, why or for what reason(s)? If not, why or for what reason? Not afraid at all.
28. Have you been in a position where you were in a relationship or engaged to please others, even though, you knew in your heart that was not the right person for you? Yes.
29. Have you considered adopting a child(ren), foster care, or some other means, if you never give birth to any child(ren) of your own? If so, what option did you consider and why? Both.
30. Do you need healing or to come to terms with some pain(s) from the past before you can be open to getting married? No.

31. Have you ever tried online dating to find a mate? If so, what was that experience like? I have used Tinder I would say nice creativity and app but needs to be free.

32. Looking back, would you do anything differently? If so, please explain. If not, please explain. I would explore other online dating sites, who knows.

33. For those of you that want to get married, what qualities do you want in a spouse? Good manners I would say.

34. Should a woman who is at least 40 years old, (who dates), be dating for the purpose of getting married? No.

35. How are you living your best life? Exercising often and going to solo destinations.

36. Name some accomplishments, goals, or visions you aspire to complete, have completed, or are working on. Successfully completed my Ph.D.

37. Is there anything else you would like to say on this subject (being a woman who is at least 40 years old, have never been married before, with no children)? No.

1. Name: Laurel D.
2. Country: USA
3. City and/or State: Utah
4. Are you happy/satisfied with being single? No.
5. Are you happy/satisfied with not having any children? Not happy/satisfied.
6. Do you or have you ever envied other women who are married and have a child(ren)? No.
7. When you let others know that you have never been married and have no children, what was their response? What was your response to their response? I feel embarrassed most of the time.
8. What have you learned about being single, with no kids? I have learned that God gives children, and abortion is a crime,

since some people like me wish to have one, but cannot because of infertility issues.

9. What advice do you have for other women 40 and over, who have never been married and never had children? I would say 40 years is not late to start over.

10. For those of you that don't ever want to get married or have children, have you encountered any negativity or criticism about this decision? No.

11. Do you have any regrets? No.

12. Do you choose to be single, with no kids, or is it circumstantial? Please explain. Mine is circumstantial. I cannot give birth.

13. Have you ever ruined or sabotaged an opportunity to get married/engaged, because of (fear of rejection, commitment, or another reason)? No.

14. If your answer is "Yes" above please explain. N/A

15. Do you feel pressured to get married and have a family from outside sources (ex., family, church, friends, society, etc.)? No.

16. Have you ever felt embarrassed about being over 40 and never been married and no kids? Yes.

17. Have you had a conversation with God about your situation? Yes.

18. How do you feel about waiting on God to send you the right husband? I feel God has the reason as to why I cannot.

19. Do you believe you would have already been married by now? Why? How? Yes, if I was fertile.

20. Are you okay if you never get married and have children? Do you accept this? Are you content? Why? Yes, although it pains me.

21. What advice or words of wisdom would you give to other women in general (whether single or not, with kids or not)? Women should avoid being lazy. Look for what motivates them and keep going.

22. Have you ever been tempted to get married or have a child because you got tired of waiting and you felt time was running out? Give examples. No.

23. Have you been engaged or thought you were going to get married and realized it was going to be a big mistake? What happened? Never.
24. Give examples of how you respond to people who question you as to why you're not married? I just don't want to settle.
25. Have you ever thought about what it would be like to be married with children? No.
26. Have you ever sabotaged a relationship/dating because you were afraid of getting married/commitment? If so, explain. Yes. I met a guy, but he wanted kids so bad. Didn't tell him I am infertile; I just sabotaged or rather ended the relationship.
27. Are you afraid of getting married? If so, why or for what reason(s)? If not, why or for what reason? I am afraid of not being able to live to the expectations of the person I get married to.
28. Have you been in a position where you were in a relationship or engaged to please others, even though, you knew in your heart that was not the right person for you? No.
29. Have you considered adopting a child(ren), foster care, or some other means, if you never give birth to any child(ren) of your own? If so, what option did you consider and why? Adopting is a great alternative.
30. Do you need healing or to come to terms with some pain(s) from the past before you can be open to getting married? No.
31. Have you ever tried online dating to find a mate? If so, what was that experience like? Never.
32. Looking back, would you do anything differently? If so, please explain. If not, please explain. Nothing.
33. For those of you that want to get married, what qualities do you want in a spouse? N/A
34. Should a woman who is at least 40 years old, (who dates), be dating for the purpose of getting married? No.
35. How are you living your best life? Vacations and road trips.
36. Name some accomplishments, goals, or visions you aspire to complete, have completed, or are working on. (Lol) I got out of a pandemic!

37. Is there anything else you would like to say on this subject (being a woman who is at least 40 years old, have never been married before, with no children)? N/A

1. Name: Olivia Z.
2. Country: USA
3. City and/or State: Denver
4. Are you happy/satisfied with being single? Maybe.
5. Are you happy/satisfied with not having any children? Yes, I am happy/satisfied.
6. Do you or have you ever envied other women who are married and have a child(ren)? No.
7. When you let others know that you have never been married and have no children, what was their response? What was your response to their response? Most people say I am lying.
8. What have you learned about being single, with no kids? I don't need a guy to make me happy.
9. What advice do you have for other women 40 and over, who have never been married and never had children? There's more to life than love.
10. For those of you that don't ever want to get married or have children, have you encountered any negativity or criticism about this decision? No.
11. Do you have any regrets? No.
12. Do you choose to be single, with no kids, or is it circumstantial? Please explain. I used to be the girl who always had a boyfriend and wanted nothing more than to settle down into a comfortable long-term relationship. It wasn't necessarily because I couldn't be without my own—I really just loved being in love. That changed not long ago, and now I've been single.

13. Have you ever ruined or sabotaged an opportunity to get married/engaged, because of (fear of rejection, commitment, or another reason)? No.

14. If your answer is "Yes" above please explain. N/A

15. Do you feel pressured to get married and have a family from outside sources (ex., family, church, friends, society, etc.)? No.

16. Have you ever felt embarrassed about being over 40 and never been married and no kids? No.

17. Have you had a conversation with God about your situation? Maybe.

18. How do you feel about waiting on God to send you the right husband? Not sure.

19. Do you believe you would have already been married by now? Why? How? Not really.

20. Are you okay if you never get married and have children? Do you accept this? Are you content? Why? Yes, I'm a total catch.

21. What advice or words of wisdom would you give to other women in general (whether single or not, with kids or not)? Have a purpose. Reach your goals and have focus.

22. Have you ever been tempted to get married or have a child because you got tired of waiting and you felt time was running out? Give examples. Never.

23. Have you been engaged or thought you were going to get married and realized it was going to be a big mistake? What happened? No.

24. Give examples of how you respond to people who question you as to why you're not married? Goals, life, and purpose. Marriage later.

25. Have you ever thought about what it would be like to be married with children? No.

26. Have you ever sabotaged a relationship/dating because you were afraid of getting married/commitment? If so, explain. Many times.

27. Are you afraid of getting married? If so, why or for what reason(s)? If not, why or for what reason? Yes, and not living according to my purpose.

28. Have you been in a position where you were in a relationship or engaged to please others, even though, you knew in your heart that was not the right person for you? No.
29. Have you considered adopting a child(ren), foster care, or some other means, if you never give birth to any child(ren) of your own? If so, what option did you consider and why? Foster care.
30. Do you need healing or to come to terms with some pain(s) from the past before you can be open to getting married? Maybe.
31. Have you ever tried online dating to find a mate? If so, what was that experience like? Never.
32. Looking back, would you do anything differently? If so, please explain. If not, please explain. Blast from the past.
33. For those of you that want to get married, what qualities do you want in a spouse? Visionary and goal oriented, also supportive of my goals.
34. Should a woman who is at least 40 years old, (who dates), be dating for the purpose of getting married? Yes.
35. How are you living your best life? I really enjoy the occasional wild night out.
36. Name some accomplishments, goals, or visions you aspire to complete, have completed, or are working on. What can I say—I believe I have achieved half of my goals in life (nice car, nice home, etc.).
37. Is there anything else you would like to say on this subject (being a woman who is at least 40 years old, have never been married before, with no children)? No.

1. Name: Ella W.
2. Country: UK
3. City and/or State: London
4. Are you happy/satisfied with being single? No.
5. Are you happy/satisfied with not having any children? Not happy/satisfied.
6. Do you or have you ever envied other women who are married and have a child(ren)? Yes.
7. When you let others know that you have never been married and have no children, what was their response? What was your response to their response? They make fun of me, and I am used to it. Nowadays I don't even respond.
8. What have you learned about being single, with no kids? That I came in this world alone and I will leave alone.
9. What advice do you have for other women 40 and over, who have never been married and never had children? Do not take marriage so seriously.
10. For those of you that don't ever want to get married or have children, have you encountered any negativity or criticism about this decision? No.
11. Do you have any regrets? No.
12. Do you choose to be single, with no kids, or is it circumstantial? Please explain. It is circumstantial.
13. Have you ever ruined or sabotaged an opportunity to get married/engaged, because of (fear of rejection, commitment, or another reason)? No.
14. If your answer is "Yes" above please explain. N/A
15. Do you feel pressured to get married and have a family from outside sources (ex., family, church, friends, society, etc.)? No.
16. Have you ever felt embarrassed about being over 40 and never been married and no kids? No.

17. Have you had a conversation with God about your situation? No.
18. How do you feel about waiting on God to send you the right husband? God's timing is the best.
19. Do you believe you would have already been married by now? Why? How? (No answer)
20. Are you okay if you never get married and have children? Do you accept this? Are you content? Why? If that is the will of God, so be it.
21. What advice or words of wisdom would you give to other women in general (whether single or not, with kids or not)? (No answer)
22. Have you ever been tempted to get married or have a child because you got tired of waiting and you felt time was running out? Give examples. No.
23. Have you been engaged or thought you were going to get married and realized it was going to be a big mistake? What happened? Yes, long story (maybe for another day).
24. Give examples of how you respond to people who question you as to why you're not married? Why should I be accountable for my personal decisions?
25. Have you ever thought about what it would be like to be married with children? No.
26. Have you ever sabotaged a relationship/dating because you were afraid of getting married/commitment? If so, explain. No, I have been sabotaged.
27. Are you afraid of getting married? If so, why or for what reason(s)? If not, why or for what reason? Yes.
28. Have you been in a position where you were in a relationship or engaged to please others, even though, you knew in your heart that was not the right person for you? No.
29. Have you considered adopting a child(ren), foster care, or some other means, if you never give birth to any child(ren) of your own? If so, what option did you consider and why? Foster care.

30. Do you need healing or to come to terms with some pain(s) from the past before you can be open to getting married? Maybe.
31. Have you ever tried online dating to find a mate? If so, what was that experience like? Never.
32. Looking back, would you do anything differently? If so, please explain. If not, please explain. I can't change what happened. What happened is just a memory.
33. For those of you that want to get married, what qualities do you want in a spouse? He's willing to put the work in.
34. Should a woman who is at least 40 years old, (who dates), be dating for the purpose of getting married? No.
35. How are you living your best life? I go to social events a lot, and this makes me happy.
36. Name some accomplishments, goals, or visions you aspire to complete, have completed, or are working on. (No answer)
37. Is there anything else you would like to say on this subject (being a woman who is at least 40 years old, have never been married before, with no children)? N/A

1. Name: Victoria A.
2. Country: USA
3. City and/or State: New York
4. Are you happy/satisfied with being single? No.
5. Are you happy/satisfied with not having any children? Not happy/satisfied.
6. Do you or have you ever envied other women who are married and have a child(ren)? No.
7. When you let others know that you have never been married and have no children, what was their response? What was your response to their response? I get responses that are hurtful, but I am a strong woman.

8. What have you learned about being single, with no kids? I have learned that it is absolutely okay to be single.

9. What advice do you have for other women 40 and over, who have never been married and never had children? To build self-esteem and self-actualization and love for yourself.

10. For those of you that don't ever want to get married or have children, have you encountered any negativity or criticism about this decision? Yes.

11. Do you have any regrets? No.

12. Do you choose to be single, with no kids, or is it circumstantial? Please explain. By choice I choose to be single instead of centering my life on someone or something that may not be around as long as you.

13. Have you ever ruined or sabotaged an opportunity to get married/engaged, because of (fear of rejection, commitment, or another reason)? No.

14. If your answer is "Yes" above please explain. No.

15. Do you feel pressured to get married and have a family from outside sources (ex., family, church, friends, society, etc.)? No.

16. Have you ever felt embarrassed about being over 40 and never been married and no kids? Yes.

17. Have you had a conversation with God about your situation? Yes.

18. How do you feel about waiting on God to send you the right husband? I believe God has a perfect life plan for me.

19. Do you believe you would have already been married by now? Why? How? No.

20. Are you okay if you never get married and have children? Do you accept this? Are you content? Why? Yes, I am okay and considering foster care.

21. What advice or words of wisdom would you give to other women in general (whether single or not, with kids or not)? It's ok to be single till you're ok with it. Even if you're upset because of singlehood, have a valid reason to be upset about it. Just because your friends tease you shouldn't affect you. You're single and that's your life, no person in this world has a right to

make fun of it. And the ones who make fun of it, are not worth you, because they can't understand you.

22. Have you ever been tempted to get married or have a child because you got tired of waiting and you felt time was running out? Give examples. No.

23. Have you been engaged or thought you were going to get married and realized it was going to be a big mistake? What happened? Never.

24. Give examples of how you respond to people who question you as to why you're not married? I get bullied quite often and I find it okay to get bullied. I normally tell them I am lucky to be single.

25. Have you ever thought about what it would be like to be married with children? Yes.

26. Have you ever sabotaged a relationship/dating because you were afraid of getting married/commitment? If so, explain. No.

27. Are you afraid of getting married? If so, why or for what reason(s)? If not, why or for what reason? Yes, I am.

28. Have you been in a position where you were in a relationship or engaged to please others, even though, you knew in your heart that was not the right person for you? No.

29. Have you considered adopting a child(ren), foster care, or some other means, if you never give birth to any child(ren) of your own? If so, what option did you consider and why? Foster care.

30. Do you need healing or to come to terms with some pain(s) from the past before you can be open to getting married? No.

31. Have you ever tried online dating to find a mate? If so, what was that experience like? So glad I got off the dating ship before online dating was a big thing. So glad.

32. Looking back, would you do anything differently? If so, please explain. If not, please explain. The fact that the past is merely a memory, not real (not here or now), I can change the way I remember it.

33. For those of you that want to get married, what qualities do you want in a spouse? (No answer)

34. Should a woman who is at least 40 years old, (who dates), be dating for the purpose of getting married? No.
35. How are you living your best life? (No answer)
36. Name some accomplishments, goals, or visions you aspire to complete, have completed, or are working on. Taking care of myself.
37. Is there anything else you would like to say on this subject (being a woman who is at least 40 years old, have never been married before, with no children)? (No answer).

1. Name: Susie B.
2. Country: USA
3. City and/or State: Charlotte
4. Are you happy/satisfied with being single? Yes.
5. Are you happy/satisfied with not having any children? Yes, I am happy/satisfied.
6. Do you or have you ever envied other women who are married and have a child(ren)? Yes.
7. When you let others know that you have never been married and have no children, what was their response? What was your response to their response? I am self-confident and I normally have no issues. I receive mixed responses and I am okay with that.
8. What have you learned about being single, with no kids? I learned that if you don't take charge of your mental health, it can affect you if you are single.
9. What advice do you have for other women 40 and over, who have never been married and never had children? It's never too late to get married.
10. For those of you that don't ever want to get married or have children, have you encountered any negativity or criticism about this decision? No.
11. Do you have any regrets? Maybe.

12. Do you choose to be single, with no kids, or is it circumstantial? Please explain. By choice.
13. Have you ever ruined or sabotaged an opportunity to get married/engaged, because of (fear of rejection, commitment, or another reason)? No.
14. If your answer is "Yes" above please explain. N/A
15. Do you feel pressured to get married and have a family from outside sources (ex., family, church, friends, society, etc.)? No.
16. Have you ever felt embarrassed about being over 40 and never been married and no kids? Maybe.
17. Have you had a conversation with God about your situation? No.
18. How do you feel about waiting on God to send you the right husband? No.
19. Do you believe you would have already been married by now? Why? How? Yes.
20. Are you okay if you never get married and have children? Do you accept this? Are you content? Why? All is well.
21. What advice or words of wisdom would you give to other women in general (whether single or not, with kids or not)? When one does not sow during the period that one is supposed to sow, one gets nothing during the harvest time.
22. Have you ever been tempted to get married or have a child because you got tired of waiting and you felt time was running out? Give examples. Never.
23. Have you been engaged or thought you were going to get married and realized it was going to be a big mistake? What happened? Truth be told my first and true love was my college sweetheart. We parted ways after graduation.
24. Give examples of how you respond to people who question you as to why you're not married? I tell them we can discuss work instead.
25. Have you ever thought about what it would be like to be married with children? Yes.

26. Have you ever sabotaged a relationship/dating because you were afraid of getting married/commitment? If so, explain. Not yet.

27. Are you afraid of getting married? If so, why or for what reason(s)? If not, why or for what reason? I am not afraid but not prepared.

28. Have you been in a position where you were in a relationship or engaged to please others, even though, you knew in your heart that was not the right person for you? No.

29. Have you considered adopting a child(ren), foster care, or some other means, if you never give birth to any child(ren) of your own? If so, what option did you consider and why? Adoption.

30. Do you need healing or to come to terms with some pain(s) from the past before you can be open to getting married? Maybe.

31. Have you ever tried online dating to find a mate? If so, what was that experience like? Yes, it was nice.

32. Looking back, would you do anything differently? If so, please explain. If not, please explain. Nothing I would do as the past is the past.

33. For those of you that want to get married, what qualities do you want in a spouse? Humility is key.

34. Should a woman who is at least 40 years old, (who dates), be dating for the purpose of getting married? No.

35. How are you living your best life? Swimming, gym and of course eating well.

36. Name some accomplishments, goals, or visions you aspire to complete, have completed, or are working on. Enrolled for a master's degree recently.

37. Is there anything else you would like to say on this subject (being a woman who is at least 40 years old, have never been married before, with no children)? No.

1. Name: Violet D.
2. Country: UK
3. City and/or State: Sheffield
4. Are you happy/satisfied with being single? Yes.
5. Are you happy/satisfied with not having any children? Yes, I am happy/satisfied.
6. Do you or have you ever envied other women who are married and have a child(ren)? No.
7. When you let others know that you have never been married and have no children, what was their response? What was your response to their response? I am ridiculed and I don't feel good.
8. What have you learned about being single, with no kids? That if you want to go far—go alone.
9. What advice do you have for other women 40 and over, who have never been married and never had children? Be kind—always—and accept nothing less from people you allow in your life. Period.
10. For those of you that don't ever want to get married or have children, have you encountered any negativity or criticism about this decision? No.
11. Do you have any regrets? No.
12. Do you choose to be single, with no kids, or is it circumstantial? Please explain. By choice to pursue my goals.
13. Have you ever ruined or sabotaged an opportunity to get married/engaged, because of (fear of rejection, commitment, or another reason)? No.
14. If your answer is "Yes" above please explain. N/A
15. Do you feel pressured to get married and have a family from outside sources (ex., family, church, friends, society, etc.)? No.
16. Have you ever felt embarrassed about being over 40 and never been married and no kids? No.

17. Have you had a conversation with God about your situation? Maybe.
18. How do you feel about waiting on God to send you the right husband? God is great and will give me a great person.
19. Do you believe you would have already been married by now? Why? How? Yes, if God said yes.
20. Are you okay if you never get married and have children? Do you accept this? Are you content? Why? Yes.
21. What advice or words of wisdom would you give to other women in general (whether single or not, with kids or not)? Being alone is positive. Strive for peace and calm in that and you might find you prefer to be alone. If you don't like being alone with you- -it can haunt you in relationships.
22. Have you ever been tempted to get married or have a child because you got tired of waiting and you felt time was running out? Give examples. (No answer)
23. Have you been engaged or thought you were going to get married and realized it was going to be a big mistake? What happened? (No answer)
24. Give examples of how you respond to people who question you as to why you're not married? (No answer)
25. Have you ever thought about what it would be like to be married with children? No.
26. Have you ever sabotaged a relationship/dating because you were afraid of getting married/commitment? If so, explain. Never in my life.
27. Are you afraid of getting married? If so, why or for what reason(s)? If not, why or for what reason? Yes.
28. Have you been in a position where you were in a relationship or engaged to please others, even though, you knew in your heart that was not the right person for you? Maybe.
29. Have you considered adopting a child(ren), foster care, or some other means, if you never give birth to any child(ren) of your own? If so, what option did you consider and why? Foster.
30. Do you need healing or to come to terms with some pain(s) from the past before you can be open to getting married? No.

31. Have you ever tried online dating to find a mate? If so, what was that experience like? The guy I met online. My date encouraged me to share the $100 steak for two. It was delicious, but he proceeded to pick out every single piece of fat from his mouth and made a pile of it on the side of his plate. I was so grossed out I couldn't bring myself to ask what the problem was. By the end of dinner, it looked like he'd spit out more than he'd ate.

32. Looking back, would you do anything differently? If so, please explain. If not, please explain. Nothing.

33. For those of you that want to get married, what qualities do you want in a spouse? Supportive and caring person.

34. Should a woman who is at least 40 years old, (who dates), be dating for the purpose of getting married? No.

35. How are you living your best life? Going out often and playing golf.

36. Name some accomplishments, goals, or visions you aspire to complete, have completed, or are working on. Best golf player of the year 2020 in our female group.

37. Is there anything else you would like to say on this subject (being a woman who is at least 40 years old, have never been married before, with no children)? (No answer)

1. Name: Madelyn O.
2. Country: USA
3. City and/or State: Virginia
4. Are you happy/satisfied with being single? Yes.
5. Are you happy/satisfied with not having any children? Yes, I am happy/satisfied.
6. Do you or have you ever envied other women who are married and have a child(ren)? No.
7. When you let others know that you have never been married and have no children, what was their response? What was your response to their response? Wonder how come with all the qualities I have.
8. What have you learned about being single, with no kids? I learned as much about myself less what I could have learned about myself when I was in a relationship.
9. What advice do you have for other women 40 and over, who have never been married and never had children? This is a man's world. It is unfair. Ungrateful. Unequal. You will have to fight for what is right, and by fight, I mean use your heart, head, and human spirit in getting things done. Not force, noise or violence.
10. For those of you that don't ever want to get married or have children, have you encountered any negativity or criticism about this decision? No.
11. Do you have any regrets? No.
12. Do you choose to be single, with no kids, or is it circumstantial? Please explain. Choice.
13. Have you ever ruined or sabotaged an opportunity to get married/engaged, because of (fear of rejection, commitment, or another reason)? No.
14. If your answer is "Yes" above please explain. N/A
15. Do you feel pressured to get married and have a family from outside sources (ex., family, church, friends, society, etc.)? No.

16. Have you ever felt embarrassed about being over 40 and never been married and no kids? No.
17. Have you had a conversation with God about your situation? Maybe.
18. How do you feel about waiting on God to send you the right husband? God is there for everyone, and He works with a plan.
19. Do you believe you would have already been married by now? Why? How? Yes.
20. Are you okay if you never get married and have children? Do you accept this? Are you content? Why? Okay.
21. What advice or words of wisdom would you give to other women in general (whether single or not, with kids or not)? Never trust any man. Most men look at women as objects of sex. If any man is nice to you – be cautious.
22. Have you ever been tempted to get married or have a child because you got tired of waiting and you felt time was running out? Give examples. No.
23. Have you been engaged or thought you were going to get married and realized it was going to be a big mistake? What happened? Never.
24. Give examples of how you respond to people who question you as to why you're not married? (I say) It is a non-issue at the moment. I would rather discuss something else.
25. Have you ever thought about what it would be like to be married with children? No.
26. Have you ever sabotaged a relationship/dating because you were afraid of getting married/commitment? If so, explain. Never.
27. Are you afraid of getting married? If so, why or for what reason(s)? If not, why or for what reason? Not afraid.
28. Have you been in a position where you were in a relationship or engaged to please others, even though, you knew in your heart that was not the right person for you? Maybe.
29. Have you considered adopting a child(ren), foster care, or some other means, if you never give birth to any child(ren) of your own? If so, what option did you consider and why? Adopting yes.

30. Do you need healing or to come to terms with some pain(s) from the past before you can be open to getting married? No.

31. Have you ever tried online dating to find a mate? If so, what was that experience like? I've been trying online dating for a few months now – mostly Tinder but also OkCupid and Bumble. It's been an interesting experience.

32. Looking back, would you do anything differently? If so, please explain. If not, please explain. None.

33. For those of you that want to get married, what qualities do you want in a spouse? (No answer)

34. Should a woman who is at least 40 years old, (who dates), be dating for the purpose of getting married? No.

35. How are you living your best life? Exploring different parts of the world.

36. Name some accomplishments, goals, or visions you aspire to complete, have completed, or are working on. I have travelled over 50 countries.

37. Is there anything else you would like to say on this subject (being a woman who is at least 40 years old, have never been married before, with no children)? (No answer)

1. Name: Mercy L.
2. Country: United States
3. City and/or State: Durham
4. Are you happy/satisfied with being single? Maybe.
5. Are you happy/satisfied with not having any children? Not happy/satisfied.
6. Do you or have you ever envied other women who are married and have a child(ren)? Yes.
7. When you let others know that you have never been married and have no children, what was their response? What was your response to their response? Wow. Why not.

8. What have you learned about being single, with no kids? It has its good moments especially with Covid.

9. What advice do you have for other women 40 and over, who have never been married and never had children? Learn to be your own best friend.

10. For those of you that don't ever want to get married or have children, have you encountered any negativity or criticism about this decision? Yes.

11. Do you have any regrets? Yes.

12. Do you choose to be single, with no kids, or is it circumstantial? Please explain. I wanted to be married before I became pregnant.

13. Have you ever ruined or sabotaged an opportunity to get married/engaged, because of (fear of rejection, commitment, or another reason)? No.

14. If your answer is "Yes" above please explain. N/A

15. Do you feel pressured to get married and have a family from outside sources (ex., family, church, friends, society, etc.)? No.

16. Have you ever felt embarrassed about being over 40 and never been married and no kids? Maybe.

17. Have you had a conversation with God about your situation? Yes.

18. How do you feel about waiting on God to send you the right husband? Ok. I want God to send me my mate.

19. Do you believe you would have already been married by now? Why? How? Yes, it was my dream.

20. Are you okay if you never get married and have children? Do you accept this? Are you content? Why? Yes, God knows what is best. I am learning to be content.

21. What advice or words of wisdom would you give to other women in general (whether single or not, with kids or not)? Do what makes you happy.

22. Have you ever been tempted to get married or have a child because you got tired of waiting and you felt time was running out? Give examples. No. Time has run out to have children.

23. Have you been engaged or thought you were going to get married and realized it was going to be a big mistake? What happened? No.

24. Give examples of how you respond to people who question you as to why you're not married? God has someone special.

25. Have you ever thought about what it would be like to be married with children? Yes.

26. Have you ever sabotaged a relationship/dating because you were afraid of getting married/commitment? If so, explain. No.

27. Are you afraid of getting married? If so, why or for what reason(s)? If not, why or for what reason? No, it would be another journey.

28. Have you been in a position where you were in a relationship or engaged to please others, even though, you knew in your heart that was not the right person for you? No.

29. Have you considered adopting a child(ren), foster care, or some other means, if you never give birth to any child(ren) of your own? If so, what option did you consider and why? I wanted a newborn, and I would have to do a private adoption. It was too expensive.

30. Do you need healing or to come to terms with some pain(s) from the past before you can be open to getting married? No.

31. Have you ever tried online dating to find a mate? If so, what was that experience like? Yes, I met someone very special. He died 2 years later due to cancer.

32. Looking back, would you do anything differently? If so, please explain. If not, please explain. No, I would keep trusting God.

33. For those of you that want to get married, what qualities do you want in a spouse? Knows God, studies the Word, prays, kind, can cook.

34. Should a woman who is at least 40 years old, (who dates), be dating for the purpose of getting married? No.

35. How are you living your best life? DOING WHAT I LIKE.

36. Name some accomplishments, goals, or visions you aspire to complete, have completed, or are working on. Losing weight.

37. Is there anything else you would like to say on this subject (being a woman who is at least 40 years old, have never been married before, with no children)? (No answer)

1. Name: Autumn P.
2. Country: USA
3. City and/or State: Farmington, UT
4. Are you happy/satisfied with being single? Yes.
5. Are you happy/satisfied with not having any children? Yes, I am happy/satisfied.
6. Do you or have you ever envied other women who are married and have a child(ren)? NO.
7. When you let others know that you have never been married and have no children, what was their response? What was your response to their response? They are usually surprised, seem to feel bad and I let them know I am quite happy.
8. What have you learned about being single, with no kids? Life is amazing and freeing, with so much more flexibility than people with kids.
9. What advice do you have for other women 40 and over, who have never been married and never had children? Live your life! Enjoy, do all the things you won't be able to do if/when that happens.
10. For those of you that don't ever want to get married or have children, have you encountered any negativity or criticism about this decision? Yes.
11. Do you have any regrets? No.
12. Do you choose to be single, with no kids, or is it circumstantial? Please explain. Totally a choice.
13. Have you ever ruined or sabotaged an opportunity to get married/engaged, because of (fear of rejection, commitment, or another reason)? Yes.

14. If your answer is "Yes" above please explain. I have turned down or "ran away" from opportunities to get married, simply because I don't want to.

15. Do you feel pressured to get married and have a family from outside sources (ex., family, church, friends, society, etc.)? Yes.

16. Have you ever felt embarrassed about being over 40 and never been married and no kids? No.

17. Have you had a conversation with God about your situation? Maybe.

18. How do you feel about waiting on God to send you the right husband? I don't care if he does or not, I'm not "waiting around" for anybody.

19. Do you believe you would have already been married by now? Why? How? I could have if I wanted to.

20. Are you okay if you never get married and have children? Do you accept this? Are you content? Why? Yes! I would prefer it. I love my life the way it is.

21. What advice or words of wisdom would you give to other women in general (whether single or not, with kids or not)? Do what you want, don't wait around for other people to "complete" your life. You are whole and complete and valuable just the way you are. Don't rely on things you can't control to make you happy. Don't give in to peer pressure if it's not something you want in your life.

22. Have you ever been tempted to get married or have a child because you got tired of waiting and you felt time was running out? Give examples. No.

23. Have you been engaged or thought you were going to get married and realized it was going to be a big mistake? What happened? Almost thought about getting married, tried to want it but I couldn't. I knew it wouldn't last.

24. Give examples of how you respond to people who question you as to why you're not married? Because I don't want to, never really have. I enjoy being single.

25. Have you ever thought about what it would be like to be married with children? I don't like to think about it for long.

26. Have you ever sabotaged a relationship/dating because you were afraid of getting married/commitment? If so, explain. Sort of, I have tried to scare guys away that want to get married. Even when I'm honest with them upfront they don't seem to believe me or take me seriously.

27. Are you afraid of getting married? If so, why or for what reason(s)? If not, why or for what reason? Maybe, I think I have trust issues. I don't necessarily believe it would last for one reason or another so the only way to avoid divorce is to not get married.

28. Have you been in a position where you were in a relationship or engaged to please others, even though, you knew in your heart that was not the right person for you? Maybe.

29. Have you considered adopting a child(ren), foster care, or some other means, if you never give birth to any child(ren) of your own? If so, what option did you consider and why? Nope.

30. Do you need healing or to come to terms with some pain(s) from the past before you can be open to getting married? Maybe.

31. Have you ever tried online dating to find a mate? If so, what was that experience like? No.

32. Looking back, would you do anything differently? If so, please explain. If not, please explain. I maybe wouldn't have dated someone with kids but that's also how I knew for sure I didn't want that.

33. For those of you that want to get married, what qualities do you want in a spouse? (No answer)

34. Should a woman who is at least 40 years old, (who dates), be dating for the purpose of getting married? No.

35. How are you living your best life? Doing whatever I want.

36. Name some accomplishments, goals, or visions you aspire to complete, have completed, or are working on. I started a business, I travel, and try to serve others.

37. Is there anything else you would like to say on this subject (being a woman who is at least 40 years old, have never been married before, with no children)? I wish it was more normal and accepted. I wish people believed that it is possible and ok to not

want to and that we are just as valuable as any wife or mother. It's a very big personal choice that no one should be pressured into.

1. Name: MiMi T.
2. Country: USA
3. City or State: Dallas, TX
4. Are you happy/satisfied with being single? Yes.
5. Are you happy/satisfied with not having any children? Yes, I am happy/satisfied.
6. Do you or have you ever envied other women who are married and have a child(ren)? Only in that I always thought I'd have a loving husband, and not do life alone; I know it doesn't turn out that way of many women (lots of divorce).
7. When you let others know that you have never been married and have no children, what was their response? What was your response to their response? It's varied over the years from disbelief to expression of surprise or perplexion.
8. What have you learned about being single, with no kids? It's a long journey letting go of the dream of how I thought life would turn out. Loneliness can be the biggest challenge in a couples, family-oriented world.
9. What advice do you have for other women 40 and over, who have never been married and never had children? Strive not to feel like you have less than or are not whole just because you don't have the husband, family etc. that has been normal for others. The grass isn't greener, it's just a different kind of grass.
10. For those of you that don't ever want to get married or have children, have you encountered any negativity or criticism about this decision? Yes.
11. Do you have any regrets? Maybe.
12. Do you choose to be single, with no kids, or is it circumstantial? Please explain. It's circumstantial and choice. I've continued to

choose not to marry a man (various) because they would eventually hold me back from the things that are the most important to me.

13. Have you ever ruined or sabotaged an opportunity to get married/engaged, because of (fear of rejection, commitment, or another reason)? No.

14. If your answer is "Yes" above please explain. N/A

15. Do you feel pressured to get married and have a family from outside sources (ex., family, church, friends, society, etc.)? Maybe.

16. Have you ever felt embarrassed about being over 40 and never been married and no kids? Yes.

17. Have you had a conversation with God about your situation? Yes.

18. How do you feel about waiting on God to send you the right husband? That has always been my stance. If I don't feel that the man and I are spiritually equal or have the same passion and goals to serve God, it is not a marital match. This is after much prayer.

19. Do you believe you would have already been married by now? Why? How? If I look at the relationships I've had, and the circumstances that have impacted the trajectory of my life, the answer is no. Otherwise, the right man would have come into my life.

20. Are you okay if you never get married and have children? Do you accept this? Are you content? Why? Yes. Loneliness challenges this sometimes. I only want to be where and with whom God places me.

21. What advice or words of wisdom would you give to other women in general (whether single or not, with kids or not)? (No answer)

22. Have you ever been tempted to get married or have a child because you got tired of waiting and you felt time was running out? Give examples. I have tried to find someone—tried to "make someone fit" but never moved away from what was essential for me.

23. Have you been engaged or thought you were going to get married and realized it was going to be a big mistake? What happened? Yes. After always seeking God in each relationship,

though painful, I knew the person was not a good long-term match.

24. Give examples of how you respond to people who question you as to why you're not married? I don't feel the need to explain. Depending on what they ask...I give the shortest answer I can.

25. Have you ever thought about what it would be like to be married with children? Yes, but it isn't very productive to dwell there.

26. Have you ever sabotaged a relationship/dating because you were afraid of getting married/commitment? If so, explain. (No answer)

27. Are you afraid of getting married? If so, why or for what reason(s)? If not, why or for what reason? It's not a matter of fear, but rather if I find that "right" connection with someone.

28. Have you been in a position where you were in a relationship or engaged to please others, even though, you knew in your heart that was not the right person for you? No.

29. Have you considered adopting a child(ren), foster care, or some other means, if you never give birth to any child(ren) of your own? If so, what option did you consider and why? No.

30. Do you need healing or to come to terms with some pain(s) from the past before you can be open to getting married? No.

31. Have you ever tried online dating to find a mate? If so, what was that experience like? Yes. Met lots of guys, went out a lot. Was saddened by the state of over-50 single men in our culture.

32. Looking back, would you do anything differently? If so, please explain. If not, please explain. No.

33. For those of you that want to get married, what qualities do you want in a spouse? I want a spiritual match foremost, and the rest is secondary.

34. Should a woman who is at least 40 years old, (who dates), be dating for the purpose of getting married? No.

35. How are you living your best life? I strive to be at peace with my life, past and present. I strive to trust God and not get into confusion or feeling like I'm missing out. I gave my best to my

career as a schoolteacher (now retired) and now hope to make a difference in other's life through volunteering.

36. Name some accomplishments, goals, or visions you aspire to complete, have completed, or are working on. Had a 30-year career as a Deaf Education Teacher. Involved at my church. Training to be a biblical counselor. Learning about many different facets of life through my volunteering. All my learning continues to show me that I have a blessed life-and don't wish I had someone else's life.

37. Is there anything else you would like to say on this subject (being a woman who is at least 40 years old, have never been married before, with no children)? This is a difficult world we live in. Not getting married (if that's how you envisioned your life) can be a very disappointing, painful reality. This can dim the goodness of one's life and in some ways rob a woman of enjoying life for what it is, single women with no kids need to be connected with each other so as to realize that being married with kids is not the only good life! I think if over the many years I knew lots of women like me, I'd have felt better. To learn how others have made it and found happiness would have helped me thru the hard years. The culture misleads us to feel less than, or like our life isn't as meaningful! I am trying to remember that life is short, and to not let the little stuff get me down. I'm healthy, retired, and have good friends. I don't want to waste more time feeling disappointed by things I cannot change or that didn't happen for me. I strive to enjoy my life.

1. Name: Aggie B.
2. Country: USA
3. City or State: St. Petersburg, Florida
4. Are you happy/satisfied with being single? Yes.
5. Are you happy/satisfied with not having any children? Yes, I am happy/satisfied.
6. Do you or have you ever envied other women who are married and have a child(ren)? Sometimes.
7. When you let others know that you have never been married and have no children, what was their response? What was your response to their response? Most people tell me that I'm smart (for never being married).
8. What have you learned about being single, with no kids? I have a lot of freedom!
9. What advice do you have for other women 40 and over, who have never been married & never had children? Enjoy your life!
10. For those of you that don't ever want to get married or have children, have you encountered any negativity or criticism about this decision? (No answer)
11. Do you have any regrets? (No answer)
12. Do you choose to be single, with no kids, or is it circumstantial? Please explain. Circumstantial. Never met a good man (for me).
13. Have you ever ruined or sabotaged an opportunity to get married/engaged, because of (fear of rejection, commitment, or another reason)? No.
14. If your answer is "Yes" above please explain. N/A
15. Do you feel pressured to get married & have a family from outside sources (ex., family, church, friends, society, etc.)? No.
16. Have you ever felt embarrassed about being over 40 and never been married and no kids? No.

17. Have you had a conversation with God about your situation? No.
18. How do you feel about waiting on God to send you the right husband? No answer)
19. Do you believe you would have already been married by now? Why? How? If I had a good match for me.
20. Are you okay if you never get married & have children? Do you accept this? Are you content? Why? Yes, I feel that my life is full. I have great friends and family.
21. What advice or words of wisdom would you give to other women in general (whether single or not, with kids or not)? Prioritize your needs and desires.
22. Have you ever been tempted to get married or have a child because you got tired of waiting and you felt time was running out? Give examples. When I was 39, I considered adopting a child or having artificial insemination. It wasn't a good time. I was back in school for nursing and wasn't working.
23. Have you been engaged or thought you were going to get married & realized it was going to be a big mistake? What happened? I've never been engaged.
24. Give examples of how you respond to people who question you as to why you're not married? I usually say that I don't have one reason why I haven't been married. I was focusing on other things (my career), moved to other states where I didn't know anyone, dated a lot of men that weren't good for me.
25. Have you ever thought about what it would be like to be married with children? Yes. Now I can imagine it.
26. Have you ever sabotaged a relationship/dating because you were afraid of getting married/commitment? If so, explain. No.
27. Are you afraid of getting married? If so, why or for what reason(s)? If not, why or for what reason? I used to be afraid I would marry the wrong man. Someone that didn't treat me well once we were married.
28. Have you been in a position where you were in a relationship or engaged to please others, even though, you knew in your heart that was not the right person for you? No.

29. Have you considered adopting a child(ren), foster care, or some other means, if you never give birth to any child(ren) of your own? If so, what option did you consider and why? Yes. I thought about all of those options.

30. Do you need healing or to come to terms with some pain(s) from the past before you can be open to getting married? No.

31. Have you ever tried online dating to find a mate? If so, what was that experience like? Yes. I'm currently active on a few dating sites. It's a good way to meet people that I wouldn't otherwise.

32. Looking back, would you do anything differently? If so, please explain. If not, please explain. I would have made better choices in dating.

33. For those of you that want to get married, what qualities do you want in a spouse? Someone responsible, kind, affectionate, fun, compassionate, loyal, and honest.

34. Should a woman who is at least 40 years old, (who dates), be dating for the purpose of getting married? No.

35. How are you living your best life? I strive to be at peace with my life, past and present. I travel, go to festivals and events, have very good friends and family.

36. Name some accomplishments, goals, or visions you aspire to complete, have completed, or are working on. I went back to school for nursing. I did travel nursing for three and a half years and got to experience more of my country.

37. Is there anything else you would like to say on this subject (being a woman who is at least 40 years old, have never been married before, with no children)? (No answer)

AFTERTHOUGHT

I hope you've gained some insight on this very taboo topic of women. My goal is talk about or bring to the forefront this marvelous group of women. Hey! We're here! We have wonderful lives that we enjoy! Yes, there are some women who want to be married with kids, but you know what? At the end of the day, these women push forward and take life day by day!
As one of these women who is a part of this group, I feel blessed, grateful, and unique. Shedding light on this group of women has provided a little insight into how these women feel. I feel a sense of community among these other women. It's almost like a secret society.
Women in this group have their highs and lows like anyone else. However, in a world where many times, that appears to epitomize being married and having kids, it's very refreshing to know that there are women who haven't for whatever reason, fallen into the traditional way of life, but are taking what life has given them and going forward to become their best. Will some of these women feel bad for not having their own family: Yes! But guess what, they have not given up hope. Just because these women are not married with kids by 40 does not mean that it will never happen. These days, more women are marrying later and having children later (through various means). But in the meantime, they are working on themselves, pursuing their vision, building worthy relationships, and simply enjoying their lives.
I, as the writer of this book, as well as a woman who is over 40, have never been married before, with no children, am very happy with my life, and have peace with who I am. I realize that everyone has their own path to walk. I am going to walk mine happily, boldly, and unapologetically!

For those of you super women who are at least 40 years old, have never been married, and with no children and you want to be a part of an exclusive community, you can join my private Facebook group: *www.facebook.com/groups/women40andovernevermarriednochildren*

Thank You!

Bibliography

- United States Census Bureau, Decennial Censuses, 1950 to 1990, and Current Population Survey, Annual Social and Economic Supplements, 1993 to 2021.
- Rybinska, A., and Morgan, S.P. (2019) Childless expectations and childlessness over the life course. Social Force. 97(4), 1571-1602.
- *https://www.psychologytoday.com/us/blog/living-single/201908/arround-the-world-marriage-is*-declining-singles-are rising
- *https://www.statistica.com/statistics/242030/marital-status-of-the-US-population-by-sex*
- Cohn, D., and Livingstone, G. (2020, July 31). Childlessness up among all women; Down among women with advanced degrees. Pew Research Center's Social and Demographic Trends Project. *https://www.pewresearch.org/social-trends/2010/06/25 childlessness-up-among-all-women-down-among-women-with-advanced-degrees/*
- "Old Maid." Merriam-Webster.com Dictionary, Merriam-Webster, *https://www.merriam-webster.com/dictionary/old%20 maid.*
- *www.Merriam-Webster.com/dictionary/spinster.* From: "spinster definition. Merriam-Webster. Retrieved 5 June 2014.

www.ingramcontent.com/pod-product-compliance
Lightning Source LLC
LaVergne TN
LVHW011932070526
838202LV00054B/4596